Golf
Anecdotes

Author Bio

Richard Stafford is a freelance sports writer and broadcaster who has spent many years following the major tours of the world, and has reported from all the great golf championships.

He is also the author of a golf instruction book, written in conjunction with the late Peter Oosterhuis.

First published in 2025
Exclusive edition for Allsorted Ltd WD19 4BG U.K.

ISBN 9781915902900

Printed in China

Golf Anecdotes

Great players ✳ True stories

Clothbound Collections

ALLSORTED.

Introduction

The great Bobby Jones perfectly summed up the capricious nature of golf when he said, "Golf is the closest game to the game we call life. You get bad breaks from good shots; you get good breaks from bad shots – but you have to play the ball where it lies."

From the middle of the 15th century, men and women have tried to manoeuvre a little white ball into a 4.25-inch hole; a task which, at times, has reduced everyone, even the greatest in the game, to gibbering wrecks.

In this collection of stories, you will learn about the inspirational, the heartbreaking, the poignant, and the funniest golfing tales from 100 of the greatest players, from Azinger to Zoeller, from Woods to Whitworth; but the anecdotes are not arranged alphabetically, instead rather loosely, so the reader can dip in and out and "play them as they lie". Why was Arnold Palmer followed by an "army"? What accident did Seve Ballesteros have with a piece of fruit cake? What happened when Gary Player met Elvis? Why did Annika Sörenstam deliberately throw a tournament?

These stories shine a light into the unseen corners of the lives and careers of the game's immortals. This not only gives us a greater understanding of what drove them to their glittering successes – and, in some cases, crushing failures – but also allows us a glimpse of how they lived their lives away from the course.

There is something within each and every anecdote that will have even the most ardent golf fans saying, "I never knew that."

So sit back, delve in and get lost in these tales from the golfing greats.

Jack Nicklaus

Born 1940

The Concession

"I don't believe you would have missed that, but I'd never give you the opportunity in these circumstances." These words remain perhaps the most famous ever spoken by one golfer to another directly after the heat of battle.

Jack Nicklaus' concession of a short, but very missable, putt to Tony Jacklin on the 18th green of the very final match in the 1969 Ryder Cup at Royal Birkdale is seen as one of the greatest acts of sportsmanship in golf.

Had Jacklin missed, the USA would have won – again. Instead, the cup was tied, for the first time in its history, and some of Jack's teammates were less than pleased, not least captain Sam Snead. "All the boys thought it was ridiculous to give him that putt," Snead said at the time. "We went over there to win, not to be good ol' boys."

But Jack was unrepentant. He said Jacklin, who had won the Open at Royal Lytham a few months earlier, was a good friend. "He was the first [golfing] hero England had had in a long time," he said later. "If he had missed that putt, the British press would have barbecued him."

The two have remained close friends, and about 20 years ago worked on the design of a course together in Bradenton, Florida. Its name? The Concession, of course.

Tiger Woods

Born 1975

When Tiger met Sam

Tiger Woods is not fond of sharing records. He likes to own them outright. But unless (or until) he wins another event on the PGA Tour, the history books will show that Woods and Sam Snead are tied at the top of the list of golfers with the most PGA Tour wins – with 82 apiece.

The pair played together once – in 1982, when Tiger was only six and Snead 69. Tiger, his father Earl, and Tiger's then coach Rudy Duran drove 75 miles from the Woods' home in Cypress, California, to play a two-hole exhibition with Snead at Soboba Springs, San Jacinto.

At their first hole, the par-3 17th, Tiger, whose tee shots went about 90 yards, hit the ball into a creek. Taking pity on the youngster, Snead told Tiger to pick the ball out and drop it. But Tiger refused, admitting later to feeling a little miffed at Snead's charity. Since the ball was only partially submerged, he went into the creek with an iron and knocked the ball onto the green.

Snead smiled and shook his head. "That's pretty good," he said. Tiger two-putted for a four, and then had another bogey at the last, while Snead went par-par.

There's a great picture of the two of them after the match with Snead signing the scorecard while Tiger, calmly drinking soda through a straw, watches. Tiger says he still has that scorecard.

Severiano Ballesteros

1957–2011

Distance control

The former BBC rugby commentator Ian Robertson recalled a moment of Seve Ballesteros genius during a practice round before the Open at Turnberry in 1986. Seve didn't have his usual caddie on the bag, and on one of the holes he asked how far he was from the pin. "For you, a 6-iron," came the caddie's reply. Seve said that's not what he asked and repeated the question, but he got the same answer: "I'm telling you, it's a 6-iron."

A furious Seve said, "You think I can't choose my own club?"

He then instructed his caddie to lay 14 balls out on the ground, six inches apart. "Give me driver," Seve said. He then hit his driver onto the green. "Now give me 3-wood," and once again, Seve struck the ball onto the green. He went through the whole bag – 3-iron, 4-iron, 5-iron, and so on – finding the green every time. With his pitching wedge he got down on one knee and somehow found the heart of the green, before doing the same with his sand wedge, and even his putter. "I've used every single club and put every ball on the green," Seve said to his caddie. "I'll try once more. Tell me: what is the distance from here to the pin?"

"Aye, it's 160 yards," his caddie replied. "And I think you'll find the one nearest the pin is your 6-iron."

Rory McIlroy

Born 1989

Big Time Rory

In 2010, at Quail Hollow, in Charlotte, North Carolina, Rory McIlroy hit one of the most important shots of his career. It didn't win him the tournament. The shot wasn't even on Sunday, or Saturday, but at the end of his round on Friday.

Playing the par-5 7th, his 16th, Rory was two shots over the cut line. He told himself that if he didn't make eagle he'd be spending the weekend practising at Ponte Vedra for the Players Championship the following week. His second shot, a 4-iron into the breeze from 206 yards, flew over the water and settled six feet from the pin, from where he holed for eagle. Pars at the last two holes meant he made the cut right on the number.

He was nine off the lead going into the weekend, but a best of the day third round of 66 reduced the deficit to four – and then the fireworks started. He finished on Sunday with six threes and played the last five holes in five under. A course record 62 gave him victory, his first on the PGA Tour, by four shots. Two days short of his 21st birthday, he became the youngest first-time winner on tour since Tiger Woods.

When Rory holed a 40-foot birdie putt on the 72nd green, Jim Nantz in the CBS commentary box, said, "Welcome to the big time." Which is where he's been ever since.

Ben Hogan

1912–1997

A dinner to remember

The Champions Dinner, on the eve of the Masters every
year, is one of the tournament's great traditions. It was
started by Ben Hogan. He had won the Masters in 1951
and the following year hosted a dinner for all previous
champions, calling it the Masters Club. The only firm
rule he made was that everyone wore their green jacket.

In 1962 Gary Player, as defending champion, hosted
the dinner. He was seated next to Ben and at one point
Horton Smith, the winner of the first Masters in 1934,
and then again in 1936, passed a book around for
everyone to sign.

After signing his name, Player put the book in front
of Ben who promptly sunk down onto his haunches
and dropped his head. Everyone in the room held their
breath. Then slowly Hogan raised his head again, and
taking the book slammed it down on the table.

Player said everyone jumped out of their skin. Ben said:
"Who passed this goddamn book up here?" And Smith
said, "Ben, I did. I got a junior at my club, a wonderful
young boy, and we want to encourage him to play golf and
I just thought this would be a marvellous print."

Ben fixed Smith with his steely stare and said,
"Horton, this is the Masters Club, not a goddamn
autograph-session club! Don't you ever do that again."

Player said he felt like he was back at school.

Greg Norman

Born 1955

Greg's Masters collapse

"Not even you can f**k up a six-shot lead tomorrow," said the British golf writer Peter Dobereiner to Greg Norman on the eve of the final round of the 1996 Masters. But that's precisely what he did.

Greg said he arrived at Augusta that week without much confidence in either his game or his body. He said he had issues with his back and his hip, and Peter Kostis, the CBS commentator and coach, noticed on the practice ground he was changing grip pressure from one round to the next. Greg shot 71 in the third round but was missing the ball left and right, and according to Kostis only his short game prevented it from being much worse.

On Saturday evening, Kostis told a TV colleague that Greg had been striking the ball erratically and feared Sunday would be a long day for him. The comments made their way onto air, which Greg heard. A few hours before his start time, he rang CBS to complain, which Kostis said was evidence he was "not in a good place".

There was also a suggestion a personal matter was playing on Greg's mind, something his coach Butch Harmon and caddie Tony Navarro observed on the practice ground on Sunday morning, which left Harmon wondering, "Who is this guy? This is not the guy who left last night."

Greg shot 78 in the last round, finishing five shots behind eventual champion Nick Faldo.

Ernie Els

Born 1969

Intense rivalry

At the 1996 Open at Royal Lytham, Ernie Els was
having a beer in the locker room after the prize-giving
ceremony (he had finished in a tie for second), when in
walked Tiger Woods, who had been leading amateur.
He asked Ernie what he thought of his game and
whether he was ready to turn pro. "Absolutely," replied
Ernie. He jokes now that he wishes he had told Tiger
something different.

The pair were involved in some great duels during
their careers. Their playoff in 2000 for the Mercedes
Championship, in Hawaii, was arguably the greatest in
the history of the PGA Tour. They both eagled the 72nd
hole, had matching birdies at the first playoff hole, and
then Tiger holed a 40-foot birdie putt at the second extra
hole to win. Ernie said afterwards he thought Tiger was
"a legend in the making" who'll probably be "bigger
than Elvis".

When the 2003 Presidents Cup at Fancourt, South
Africa, finished in a tie, Ernie and Tiger, the two best
golfers in the world at the time, were sent out by their
captains to contest a sudden death playoff which would
determine the destiny of the cup. Darkness called a
halt before a winner was declared, but not before they
had halved three holes, matching each other stroke for
stroke, putt for putt, under the most intense pressure.

Phil Mickelson

Born 1970

A Master thief

Phil Mickelson loves the Masters – after all, he's won it three times. But maybe the Augusta National committee is not so fond of him.

Just before the Masters in 2004, coach Dave Pelz had Phil practise a drill on Augusta's East practice range, placing towels at various yardages to help him build reference points. It worked. He won the Masters that year.

When he came back 12 months later, a sign was up on the East range, saying it was for short game practice only. Golfers are creatures of habit and Phil didn't want his routine broken. So, he waited until everyone had left the Champions Dinner and then, having parked his car on Magnolia Lane, crawled on his hands and knees beneath the magnolias and yanked up the sign. He then threw it in the boot of his SUV. He came back the next day and practised on the East range without any trouble.

In 2006, the sign had returned. So once again, after the Champions Dinner, Phil uprooted the sign. Only this time when he came back the next day, another sign had been put up. He was unaware that video cameras had been installed around the East range and footage existed of his heist, with people saying, "Look at this idiot. What's he doing?"

It means Phil's total haul from Augusta is three green jackets and two signposts.

"I would rather try a shot to win than play safe and finish second."

Phil Mickelson

Payne Stewart

1957–1999

Standing out from the crowd

In 1982, Payne Stewart was on the practice range at his
first PGA Tour event, and he took a moment to study
the line of pros warming up with him. One thing stood
out: everyone was dressed as he was in traditional golf
slacks and striped polo shirt. "Hell, we all just looked the
same," he said.

Payne wanted to look different. His father had been a
salesman who wore colourful, mismatched clothes and
he once told his son that people remembered him more
for his style choices than for what he was selling.

Payne also remembered the Australian Rodger Davis,
and his penchant for wearing plus-twos. "I thought he
looked different and neat," Payne said. He went to T.
Barry Knicker Co., in Palm Desert, California, who over
the course of Payne's career made over 200 bespoke
pairs of plus-fours, or knickers, for him. Payne later
signed a lucrative deal with the NFL to wear an outfit
in the colours of whichever team was closest to the
tournament venue.

Dressing so flamboyantly had its benefits off the
course because nobody recognized him. In 1999,
Payne was selling his house and the realtor wouldn't
tell him who was coming to view it. To his amazement,
in walked Michael Jackson. The King of Pop had no idea
who Payne was until the realtor said, "The golfer with
the funny clothes."

"Oh, I know who you are now," said Jackson.

Arnold Palmer

1929–2016

You're in the Army now

Arnold Palmer's loyal cohort of fans was known as Arnie's Army, a moniker that originated at the Masters, and named after an actual legion of soldiers.

By the late 1950s the Masters had started to be televised but it wasn't yet a popular tournament. The club wanted large galleries for the cameras, and so they offered entry at the gate for as little as $5. Tickets were given free to local schools, and to the nearby army garrison at Camp Gordon, where the Masters co-founder and chairman Cliff Roberts had been stationed for two years. The GIs would help man the leaderboards around the course.

Many of the soldiers knew little about golf, and in 1959, when Arnie was defending champion, they supported him because he had spent three years in the US Coast Guard and considered him one of their own. Dressed in army uniform, they followed him around the course. One of the back nine leaderboards referred to the presence of Arnie's Army. The following year, Arnie won his second Masters and he thanked his "army" of supporters.

Stories differ as to who first used the term "Arnie's Army". Arnie himself attributed it to Augusta's local paper, *The Chronicle*, and to a writer called Johnny Hendrix. Arnie said later, "Boy, did it ever stick! Before I finished my playing career I think every newspaper, magazine, or television station that covered golf used the phrase at least once."

Nick Faldo

Born 1957

Mimic your heroes

Nick Faldo's first Open Championship was at Royal Troon
in 1973 – as a 16-year-old spectator. He and his father
drove up to Scotland from their home in Hertfordshire,
their car packed with camping gear. Nick remembers
pulling in at a petrol station in Troon, and seeing Tony
Jacklin filling up his Rolls-Royce, with Tom Weiskopf in
the passenger seat.

They camped all week and Nick said it was so cold,
even in the day, that he wore pyjamas under his clothes.
He would go to the practice range and watch his six big
heroes every day – Arnold Palmer, Jack Nicklaus, Johnny
Miller, Tom Weiskopf, Gary Player and Lee Trevino –
and study the idiosyncrasies of their swings so he could
mimic them. At the end of the week, he went back to his
club at Welwyn Garden City and every afternoon played
an imaginary three-ball with two of these great players,
copying the shape of their shots – for example, hitting
a fade for Nicklaus, Miller and Trevino, and a draw for
Palmer, Weiskopf and Player.

Later, he told Nicklaus this is how he learned to play,
and Nicklaus said he did the same when he was young.
His coach sent him to Byron Nelson and Sam Snead to
study their swings, and he would copy them. Mimicking
his heroes, Nick said, was for him such a powerful
learning mechanism.

Annika Sörenstam

Born 1970

A woman in a man's world

When Annika Sörenstam strode onto the 1st tee of an event in Fort Worth, Texas, in May 2003 it was the biggest story in golf.

She began her round with three regulation pars and when she birdied her fourth hole her name appeared on the leaderboard. Nothing out of the ordinary for the pre-eminent player in the women's game at the time, with four majors to her name.

Except this was no ordinary golf tournament. It was the Bank of America Colonial, one of the longest-running events on the men's tour, making Annika the first woman to play a PGA Tour event in over 50 years.

Not everyone thought Annika should be there. Vijay Singh said if she wanted to play, she should come through qualifying, and threatened to pull out if he was drawn to play with her. As it was, her two rookie partners, Aaron Barber and Dean Wilson, were delighted to be in her company.

In her opening one-over-par round of 71 she hit 13 of 14 fairways (leading the field in accuracy), and 14 greens in regulation. Her 74 the next day meant she missed the cut by four strokes, but she was let down, not by her long game which stood comparison with the men, but by her putting.

It was Annika's only appearance in a men's event but for a while she led the way for other female players to follow.

Johnny Miller

Born 1947

The greatest final round in history

When the players arrived at Winged Foot, in upstate
New York, for the 1974 US Open they found rough nine
inches high. It was so thick in places it was impossible to
move the ball more than 90 yards. There was one man
they blamed for the course set-up: Johnny Miller.

The previous year Johnny shot a final round of 63 to
win the US Open at Oakmont, in Pittsburgh, arguably
the greatest round to win a major championship in
the history of golf. He brought the course to its knees,
coming from eight shots back, and the USGA wouldn't
make that mistake again. "Thanks a lot for that stinkin'
63, Miller," players said to him after their Winged
Foot humiliation.

At Oakmont 12 months earlier, Johnny thought he
was out of the championship on Sunday morning, and
so experimented on the range with a wider than usual
stance. "Who tries a new tip on Sunday at the US Open?"
he said to himself. But he thought, what the heck, I'm
not likely to win.

He birdied the first four holes and his thinking
changed. "Jeez," he said. "I'm in this." He hit 13 out of 14
fairways that afternoon, and shot at the pin on 15 holes,
leaving himself ten birdie putts of 15 feet or less.

As he was walking to the 12th tee, overnight leader
Arnold Palmer glanced at the leaderboard and said,
"Johnny Miller? Where the f**k did he come from?"

Sam Snead

1912–2002

Monkey business

Sam Snead's lifelong friend William C. Campbell, a World Golf Hall of Famer and 1964 US Amateur champion, tells a story about Sam that is hard to believe. But then, many aspects of Sam's life stretched credulity.

In 1947, Sam was playing a match against Bobby Locke in South Africa and was captivated by the squirrel monkeys that played in the trees alongside the course. Campbell says an idea came to him: to start a monkey farm back home.

So, he took two back to America with him, concealing them inside his shirt to get them through customs. Apparently, they scratched him quite badly. He wasn't going back to his home in Virginia. He was going to Augusta for the Masters, and while he was playing left them in his hotel room, which they proceeded to ruin, much to the fury of the hotel manager. He finished 22nd in the Masters that year and won $50, which we suspect he would have had to pay to the hotel to cover the damages.

When he got back home, he kept them in his basement, which his wife Audrey was less than pleased about. One of them then escaped through an open window while the other one was sadly killed when something fell on it.

Sam abandoned his monkey farm idea at this point.

José María Olazábal

Born 1966

Ollie's pep talks

When José María Olazábal arrived at Augusta in 1999 he was struggling with accuracy from the tee. The champion from five years earlier said his iron play was good, as was his touch around the greens, "but the driver," he said, "my God, it was all over the park." However, encounters that week with two former Masters champions changed his mindset.

The first encounter came after Tuesday's Champions Dinner. He was ushered into the locker room by Gary Player who pushed him against the lockers. "Look at me," Player said, pumping his chest with his fist. "Look at me. Strong like a bull. You have to believe. You have the game. You can win this again!" Player then left, leaving José María slightly bemused by the encounter.

The next day he played a practice round with his friend Seve Ballesteros, during which José María's driving was still a concern to him. Seve said, "All you have to do is put the ball in play. The rest of the game is really good. Your iron play, your putting, everything is nice. Why don't you slow down the backswing and don't try to hit it hard." José María tried to speak, but before he could, Seve interrupted him. "Do that, see how things go."

Heeding Seve's advice and inspired by Player's eccentric pep talk, José María went on to win his second green jacket.

Davis Love III

Born 1964

What goes around comes around...

Davis Love III knows this adage better than most. In 1987, he was sitting anxiously in the clubhouse at Sea Pines, Hilton Head, with a one-shot lead in the MCI Heritage Classic. It was his second season on tour, and he had yet to win. The only player that could deny him was Steve Jones, who was also winless after six years on tour. Needing a par at the last to win, Jones sliced his tee shot out of bounds and made double bogey. The title was Davis'. He said he was "pulling for Steve Jones since then".

Perhaps he was pulling too hard. Fast forward to 1996 and the US Open at Oakland Hills, Michigan, where once again Davis was in the clubhouse, a shot behind Jones and Tom Lehman, who were coming up the 18th. Davis had had a nightmare finish. He had dropped a shot at the 17th and then at the 18th three-putted from 20 feet, taking an eternity over his second putt from less than three feet. He stopped to wave some flies away from his line and then missed it left. If he was to win his first major championship, he would have to rely on history repeating itself. And although Lehman made a bogey, Jones did not make the mistake he made in South Carolina nine years earlier and calmly putted out to win the title.

"It is nothing new or original to say that golf is played one stroke at a time. But it took me many years to realize it."

Bobby Jones

Bobby Jones

1902–1971

The Bobby Slam

In 1930, Robert (Bobby) Tyre Jones Jr achieved what many at the time thought impossible: he won golf's Grand Slam, made up of the British Amateur, the Open Championship, the US Open and the US Amateur.

In the eyes of many it made Bobby the finest player, amateur or professional, of his generation, and his Grand Slam the greatest achievement in golf.

The first two legs of what was known as the Impregnable Quadrilateral were in Britain, and after two months at sea, he warmed up by captaining the American Walker Cup team, which beat Britain 10-2 at Royal St George's in Kent. Bobby took down Roger Wethered 9&8 in the second day singles.

He then won the 18-hole Golf Illustrated Gold Vase at Sunningdale, before eviscerating Wethered again, 7&6, in the final of the Amateur Championship at St Andrews.

Then it was on to Royal Liverpool where he recorded a two-stroke victory in the Open. In July, at Interlachen, Minnesota, he won the US Open, and then two months later he beat Gene Homans 8&7 to win the US Amateur at Merion, Pennsylvania, the fourth and final leg of the Grand Slam. It's reported that in the locker room afterwards he told his friend Jimmy Johnston that "the strain of golf is wrecking my health". In November, he announced his retirement at just 28. The writer Herbert Warren Wind said, "There were no worlds left for him to conquer."

Gene Sarazen

1902–1999

Stamped with an ace

On his way to winning the Masters in 1935, enabling him to complete his career Grand Slam, Gene Sarazen famously made an albatross at Augusta's 15th hole in the last round. It was known as "the shot that was heard around the world" because it helped make Augusta National and the Masters tournament what they are today.

Thirty-eight years later, in the first round of the 1973 Open at Royal Troon, a 71-year-old Gene hit another miracle shot, at the 123-yard 8th hole, otherwise known as the Postage Stamp. Gene said this hole, the shortest on the Open course rota, always haunted him. With the wind in his face and determined not to leave it short, he selected a 5-iron. The ball pitched about 20 feet short of the pin and dropped dead weight into the hole.

In what was only his second start of the year (he played the Masters in April) he went on to shoot 79. Gene, who won the Open at Prince's, in Sandwich, in 1932, said later, "I felt there was no better way to close the books on my tournament play than to make a hole-in-one on the Postage Stamp."

The next day, Gene holed out on the 8th again, this time from a greenside bunker for birdie. In two rounds, he had played the hole in a total of three shots and without even picking up his putter.

Lloyd Mangrum

1914–1973

War hero

Lloyd Mangrum was known as much for his heroism in World War II as for his golf. In his first Masters in 1940, he shot 64 in the first round, a course record that stood for 46 years. He didn't win the tournament (he finished second behind Jimmy Demaret) but it was the launchpad to him winning five times on the PGA Tour in the next two years. He turned down an offer to become professional at Fort Meade Golf Course in Maryland, choosing instead to enlist in the US Army.

During the war, before the Normandy Landings, Mangrum ripped a dollar bill in two and gave the other half to his best friend, Robert Green. They were meant to reunite the two halves in victory, but Green was killed shortly after. Mangrum carried the torn bill with him for the rest of his life. He said later, "I don't suppose any of the pro and amateur golfers who were combat soldiers, Marines or sailors will think of a three-putt green as one of the really bad troubles in life."

Lloyd was one of only two soldiers from his unit to survive the war, returning home with two Purple Heart medals and four meritorious battle stars. Despite breaking his arm in two places in a jeep crash and being wounded by shrapnel in his knee, Lloyd went on to win the 1946 US Open at Canterbury Golf Club, in Ohio.

Gary Player

Born 1935

Hip swing

In 1961, the new Masters champion Gary Player met the King – no, not Arnold Palmer. It was another king, the king of rock and roll, Elvis Presley.

After his victory, Gary was on a morning chat show on American television, and the presenter had a guitar with her in the studio. "Hand me that," Gary said, and he played a few bars of "Blue Suede Shoes" while showing off some hip movements. "You can really move," the presenter said. "Baby, I really *can* move," Gary replied. "That's my business. Dancing."

A few days later Gary got a telegram from the film producer Hal Wallis. "Elvis wants to meet you," the telegram said. So, Gary travelled to Los Angeles, where Elvis was making the movie *Blue Hawaii*. Elvis told Gary he wanted to play golf, and demonstrated his grip, which Gary said later was like "a cow giving birth to a roll of barbed wire".

Then Elvis wanted to know what the most important part of the swing was. "You gotta use those hips, man," Gary said, showing him his golf swing. "You gotta wind up with those hips and then unwind with those hips."

"The hips?" Elvis replied. "You're talking to the right man there, boy." And then he demonstrated his own take on the golf swing, with his trademark swing of the hips that had young women swooning at his concerts.

"Man, could he move those hips," Gary said.

Sergio García

Born 1980

The wrong clubs

In 2008, TaylorMade sent two sets of clubs to Sergio García's house in Spain. One was for him, and the other for his father, Victor. To the uninitiated, they might have looked the same, but they had different lies, different offsets, and, crucially, different shafts. Sergio's set were fitted with X1 shafts, and Victor's with S400 shafts.

A few weeks later, Sergio headed off to Florida to play in the Players Championship at TPC Sawgrass – although, unbeknownst to him, he took his father's clubs. Before the tournament started, since he hadn't heard from Sergio, the TaylorMade rep asked him how he was finding the irons. Sergio said he liked them.

A few days later, in windy conditions, Sergio won the tournament, beating Paul Goydos in a playoff for what, at the time, was his biggest win on American soil.

Back at TaylorMade headquarters, there was a debate among staff as to whether someone should tell Sergio he had been playing with his father's clubs but given that he had just won golf's unofficial fifth major, they decided that, in this case, ignorance was bliss.

Tom Watson

Born 1949

Losing the choker tag

Before he made his major breakthrough at the Open Championship in 1975, Tom Watson had a reputation as a bit of a choker. At the US Open at Winged Foot the previous year he held the lead after 54 holes, only to shoot a 79 on Sunday.

He said later, "I was losing a lot of shots to the right, my Achilles' heel, and you just couldn't play out of that rough. My nerves wouldn't allow me to adjust. That's what choking is – being so nervous you can't find a swing or a putting stroke you can trust."

After his round, he was having a beer in the clubhouse with John Mahaffey, commiserating with one another, when the great Byron Nelson walked in. Nelson said he knew how Tom must have been feeling. He told him he liked how he handled himself on the course and praised his golf swing. "If you ever need any help with your game, give me a call," Nelson said.

Tom said very little. He was still smarting at how poorly he had played. But two years later, Tom did call Nelson, who gave Tom the best cure for nerves. "Walk slowly, talk slowly, deliberately do everything more slowly than you normally do. It has a way of settling you down," Nelson told him. It was a piece of advice Tom would never forget and marked the beginning of a deep and lasting friendship.

"The person I fear most in the last two rounds is myself."

Tom Watson

Laura Davies

Born 1963

Practice is a chore

Laura Davies hates practising, but it hasn't stopped her from winning 87 events around the world, including 20 times on the LPGA Tour. She has four majors to her name as well, which would have been five had her success in the Women's British Open in 1986 been classified a major back then.

American golf writer Ron Sirak remembers Laura at the 2005 Chick-fil-A Charity Championship, near Atlanta, Georgia. He says she went to the practice range on a rainy first day and stood under an umbrella for 20 minutes, watching her fellow players hit balls. Then she went to the putting green and stood there for 20 minutes under her umbrella, watching. Finally, she went to the first tee, cracked one down the middle, and ended up shooting 68. "I don't practise when it's nice. Why would I hit balls in the rain?" she said later. Another time, Sirak remembers Laura being asked after a poor putting round if she was going to go to the putting green. "Why would I practise missing?" she said.

Laura has her own idiosyncrasies. At the 1996 LPGA Championship at DuPont Country Club, in Wilmington, Delaware, instead of using a conventional tee peg, Laura ripped the eraser off the top of a pencil, stuck it in the ground, and teed the ball up on that. She won the championship by a stroke, the third of her four major wins.

Craig Stadler

Born 1953

A snitch in time

In 1987, Craig Stadler became the first victim of a TV rules snitch. In the third round of the Andy Williams Open at Torrey Pines, California, Craig hit a drive under a tree on the 14th hole. He put a towel down to prevent his trousers from getting dirty and played his second shot on his knees.

The next day, Rick Schloss, the media coordinator of the event, received a phone call from a viewer, who said a player had committed a rules violation. Schloss thought, "OK, whatever. You get crazy people calling all the time about certain things." When another fan called later with the same observation and asked to speak to the commentators, Vin Scully and Lee Trevino, Schloss felt duty bound to inform a rules official.

It turned out that Craig had broken Rule 13-3, which forbids the illegal building of a stance, and only the armchair fans had spotted it. Craig was given a retrospective two-stroke penalty, and then disqualified because he had signed for the wrong score the previous day.

Eight years later, when Craig was in California for the USPGA at nearby Riviera, Schloss invited Craig back to Torrey Pines. With a team of greenkeepers, they drove out to the 14th where Craig took a chainsaw to the tree and cut it down.

From 1 January 2018, golf's governing bodies no longer allowed tournaments to field rules enquiries from armchair viewers.

Jim Furyk

Born 1970

Jim's untouchable swing

He has the funkiest swing in golf, and believe it or not, his father Mike, himself an assistant club professional, didn't want anyone tampering with it. When Jim was at high school in Pennsylvania a college coach, up on a recruiting mission, watched him play in the high school state championships. Afterwards, he took Mike and his wife Linda to dinner at a fancy steak restaurant.

The coach said how excited he was to get Jim down to his school so he could change his swing, to which Mike said, "That's exactly what I wanted to hear." The coach assumed he and Mike were on the same page, that he knew his son's swing needed changing. Mike said, "No, I don't ever want it to be changed, but you eliminated yourself from the recruiting process and I just want to thank you for doing that. And for dinner as well. He won't be coming your way."

Jim went to the University of Arizona instead, where he was twice an All-American, and in 1992 led the college golf team to their first NCAA title. He turned pro later that year and was frequently ridiculed for his dramatically upright, ugly-looking swing. He had the last laugh. He won the US Open in 2003 and then, in 2016, his unorthodox swing helped him find all but one fairway on route to a record-breaking 58 in the final round of the Travelers Championship.

Fuzzy Zoeller

Born 1951

Waving the white flag

In the final round of the US Open at Winged Foot, New York, in 1984, Fuzzy Zoeller was in a titanic tussle for the title with Greg Norman. They were both at four under playing the 72nd hole, five clear of the field. Norman was in the group ahead and had a downhill 40-foot putt, with about 15 feet of break, from just off the left fringe. Fuzzy, arms folded, watched from the middle of the fairway as Norman sank the putt. He assumed it was for birdie and said to his caddie Mike Mazzeo, "That SOB is gonna beat us." He took a white towel from his bag and waved it in mock surrender.

Only when he was about to hit did a USGA official inform Fuzzy that Norman had carved his approach shot from the middle of the 18th fairway into the stands and the putt was for par. "You're kidding!" Fuzzy replied. The stands were about 30 yards right of the green. A few minutes later, Fuzzy two-putted to join Norman on 276. As he walked off the green, he gave his white towel to a young fan.

The next day, in the 18-hole playoff, Fuzzy was three under playing the last, eight shots clear of his rival. As he walked up onto the green, Norman waved a white towel. Fuzzy had a US Open title to add to his Masters victory five years earlier.

Jordan Spieth

Born 1993

Big bluff

Jordan Spieth was the victim of a great golfing prank in 2020. When COVID-19 brought the PGA Tour to a halt, Jordan and his wife Annie went up into the Colorado mountains for a few days. One afternoon, Jordan played with a friend at a local course, Snowmass Golf Club, just outside Aspen.

The 12th hole is a driveable par-4 played to an elevated green, which means back on the tee players cannot see their ball land. Jordan went for the green and pulled it off, his ball finishing about 20 feet from the pin. Watching by the green was local resident Shane Smith. He had heard that the three-time major champion was playing in his backyard and came out to watch.

Unseen by the players, Smith ran onto the green, picked up Jordan's ball and put it in the hole. When Jordan arrived at the green, he looked about for his ball, but to no avail. He asked Smith if he had seen it. "Oh, is that you?" Smith replied, playing dumb. "It's in the hole."

Jordan had never aced a par-4, and he started celebrating wildly. It's then that Smith came clean. "Hey, man, I was trying to be funny," he said, "but your ball finished over there. I actually put it in the hole."

Jordan took the disappointment well. He said to Smith, "You took me from the mountaintop way down to the valley."

Colin Montgomerie

Born 1963

Indecision leads to failure

Colin Montgomerie arrived for the US Open in 2006 as the best player never to have won a major. He was nearly 43, and chances were running out. He opened with an excellent 69 at Winged Foot, in upstate New York, and was three shots off the lead going into the last round. When he holed a monster birdie putt on the 17th green he had a share of the lead.

His drive down the last split the fairway. He pulled out a 6-iron for his second shot and waited for his playing partner Vijay Singh, who had driven into the left rough, to find his ball. In all, Monty waited for about ten minutes. At the last moment, he exchanged his 6-iron for a 7-iron. On commentary, Johnny Miller said, "I'm surprised he's just switched clubs when you've had ten minutes to think about it."

Monty said later, "By the time it was my turn, I was beginning to second-guess myself. Was it a 7-iron? Was it not a 6? Was it a big 7-iron or a little one?" Whatever the explanation, Monty hit the worst iron shot of his life. "What kind of shot is that?" he cried as the ball landed short and right in the thick rough.

He ended up making double bogey and lost by a shot. He left Winged Foot as he had arrived – the best player never to have won a major.

Lee Trevino

Born 1939

A Master strop

Every professional golfer would give an arm and a leg to play the Masters, right? Well, no, not all. Despite being invited, Lee Trevino chose not to play in 1970, 1971 and 1974, arguably his peak years. And when he did go, he wouldn't enter the clubhouse, changing his shoes in his car and keeping his clubs in the boot.

In 1969, he announced he wasn't coming back because the course didn't suit his eye. Lee played with a low fade, and Augusta predominately favours those that hit the ball with a high draw.

But in 2023, he explained the real reason for his no-shows. He had a blazing argument with the Masters chairman Cliff Roberts, who Lee branded a "dictator". Lee wanted to buy gallery tickets one year for some of his friends and was told by the club that he couldn't. He also claims that a security guard tried to kick his caddie, Neil Harvey, out. Super-Mex had a confrontation with Roberts in his office. "I took a disliking to the man, and he took a disliking to me," Lee said. "I didn't want to have anything to do with him."

Lee admits now that the course had nothing to do with it. "I loved Augusta," he said. "It's gorgeous." As for Augusta not suiting his game, Lee remembered that Jimmy Demaret won the Masters three times, and, like Lee, he played with a fade.

"Caddies are a breed of their own. If you shoot 66, they say: 'Man we shot 66 today.' But go out and shoot 77 and they say: 'Heck, he shot 77.'"

Lee Trevino

Bubba Watson

Born 1978

Pretty in pink

Bubba Watson is well known for the prodigious distances he hits the ball off the tee. But he is equally well known for the colour of the golf club he uses – a hot pink driver.

When he was on the Nationwide Tour, the tour a level below the regular PGA Tour, Bubba went to shaft manufacturer True Temper and said, "I want a hot pink shaft." Their response was an emphatic, "No! Who are you?"

In 2004, Bubba qualified for the US Open, which that year was being played at Shinnecock Hills. He was being watched by Matt Rollins, from club manufacturer Ping, and reps from True Temper. Rollins had said to the True Temper reps, "Just come watch him hit before you say no to the driver shaft." They gathered at the 1st hole, a 393-yard par-4, with a dogleg right, and watched Bubba drive the ball over the green, at which point Bubba remembers True Temper saying, "OK, what colour do you want your driver?" "Pink," he replied.

Despite Ping's corporate colours being black and white, Bubba's pink driver has helped raise millions for charity. Ping has sold thousands of limited-edition pink Ping G drivers, similar to the one used by Bubba, with proceeds going to the Bubba Watson Foundation.

Walter Hagen

1892–1969

The Battle of the Century

In 1926, Walter Hagen played a 72-hole exhibition match against Bobby Jones in what was dubbed The Battle of the Century. There was more at stake than bragging rights. It was a match between the world's leading amateur golfer and the world's leading professional. As Walter said, "The public consider amateurs the Galahads of golf. While I was a professional – the natural villain of the game."

It was Walter's idea. He had been trying to convince Jones to turn pro, knowing how much money they could make playing exhibitions. Over 1,000 spectators were around the 1st tee on the morning of 28 February at Jones' home course in Sarasota, Florida. But the match was something of an anti-climax. Walter was 3 up after 18 holes, and then at the par-4 6th in the second round Walter topped a shot out of the rough. The ball scuttled down the fairway, ran through a greenside bunker, up a bank and settled ten feet from the hole. From there, he made birdie to go 4 up. Jones said to himself, "I'm 4 down to a man who can miss one like that!"

Walter came home in 32 and was 8 up at halfway. A week later at Pasadena, Walter increased his lead and won 12&11. Many think the drubbing convinced Jones to shelve any idea he might have had about turning pro which would have altered the course of golfing history.

Raymond Floyd

Born 1942

Calm after the storm

On his way to the 1986 US Open at Shinnecock Hills, Long Island, Raymond Floyd and his wife Maria stopped their car on the Long Island Expressway and had a blazing row.

The previous week, Ray lost the Westchester Classic after sharing a 54-hole lead and Maria wanted to know why it happened. He didn't have an answer. "What if it happens again this week?" Maria asked. "You never do well in the US Open. What's the problem?" Ray lost his temper. He pulled over onto the hard shoulder and he and his wife went at it, reducing their three children and their nanny on the back seat to tears. When they set off again, Ray said he did some serious soul-searching, which he realized later was Maria's intention.

Historically, Ray's problem with the US Open was the courses, which he said the USGA set up to take certain players out of the game. But he loved Shinnecock. He said it was set up to favour players who were in good form – as he was.

Ray began the final round three off the lead. Walking to the 10th tee he saw Maria in the gallery. She said later she could tell from the look on Ray's face he was going to win. A birdie at the 11th briefly took him into a nine-way tie for the lead and he went on to shoot 66 and claim his one and only US Open title.

Tony Jacklin

Born 1944

Eyes on the prize

In 1970, Tony Jacklin became the first British player to win the US Open since the Scot Willie Macfarlane in 1925.

He led wire-to-wire, although Dave Hill, who finished second, garnered more publicity for his criticisms of the course at Hazeltine, Minnesota, than Tony's victory, saying all the course lacked "was 80 acres of corn and a few cows to be a good farm".

Earlier in the week, Tony played a practice round with Tom Weiskopf and Bert Yancey and left the course a little depressed because he had putted poorly. Yancey's older brother Jim had walked round with them and asked Tony if he had thought about keeping his eyes fixed on the hole while he putted. "Why would I want to do that?" Tony asked.

Jim took Tony to the putting green where he tried the drill, and after a little while something clicked. Tony said it gave him a great feel for distance, and although he didn't have the courage to adopt the method in the championship, he made sure that over every putt he gave the hole a good, long look.

When he made a long putt on the opening hole in the first round, he knew the unusual method was going to be his friend that week. And that's how it turned out. Tony won by seven shots and for a short while held both the US and Open Championship titles at the same time.

Dustin Johnson

Born 1984

Rules controversy No. 1

It's been called one of the worst rules decisions in the history of golf. In 2010, Dustin Johnson came to the 72nd hole of the USPGA Championship with a one-shot lead. He had suffered major heartbreak in June that year when he held a three-shot lead at the US Open at Pebble Beach, only to shoot 82 in the last round and finish in a tie for eighth. But now, at Whistling Straits, in Wisconsin, he seemed destined to make amends and win his first major.

His drive at the last went right into what he thought was a waste area. The course has about 1,000 sandy areas which tournament organizers classified as bunkers, even though some of them resembled patches of dirt. A notice had been pinned up in the locker room, informing players to this effect, but DJ had forgotten this. A few minutes later, he believed he was in a playoff with Martin Kaymer and Bubba Watson for the title, only to be told by a rules official that because he had grounded his club, he had incurred a two-shot penalty, meaning he missed out on the playoff which Kaymer won.

He said later, "There's Gatorade bottles, beer cans, cups, trash. Anything and everything is just sat around my ball. I never once think that I am in a bunker. I never even thought I was in sand, it just looked like dirt."

Mildred "Babe" Didrikson Zaharias

1911–1956

Beware the ailing golfer

In 1999, Associated Press named Babe Zaharias the greatest athlete of the 20th century. Although golf was the sport for which she was best known, prior to turning pro she represented the USA in three events at the 1932 Olympics in Los Angeles, winning gold medals in the 60m hurdles and the javelin, and a silver medal in the high jump.

She won 48 golf tournaments in her career, including ten major championships. The most remarkable was her last, the 1954 US Women's Open at Salem Country Club, Massachusetts. The previous year she had been diagnosed with colon cancer and had an operation, during which she was fitted with a colostomy bag.

To save energy, she limited herself to only nine holes of practice at Salem, and then shot 72 in the first round. "Man, I don't know when I've felt this good," she said afterwards. A second round 71 gave her a seven-stroke halfway lead and a 36-hole championship record. The final 36 holes were to be played on one day. With temperatures in the 80s and on a course measuring nearly 6,400 yards, people wondered if her body would hold up.

Despite doctors warning her she might never play again, Babe won by 12 shots. At the trophy presentation she revealed that lying in her hospital bed she had said a prayer. "I said please make me able to play again. I'll take care of the winning."

"Concentration comes out of a combination of confidence and hunger."

Arnold Palmer

Arnold Palmer

Chewing the grass

English golfer Lee Westwood played his first Bay
Hill Invitational, held every year at Arnold Palmer's
home club in Florida, in 1998. It was one of the first
tournaments a 24-year-old Westwood had played in
on the PGA Tour. He was in contention to win until he
dropped a handful of shots over the closing three holes
and plummeted down the leaderboard.

He was quite disconsolate walking off the 18th until
Arnie, who was always next to the green on the final day
to talk to the players as they finished, shook his hand. A
few minutes later Ernie Els won the tournament.

Westwood said he was having a few drinks in the
clubhouse when Els came in and sat next to him,
followed by Arnie a few minutes later. Arnie ordered a
neat vodka – "Arnold loved a vodka," Lee remembers –
and asked if he could join them.

It then occurred to Arnie who Westwood was, and
how the wheels had come off at the end of his round. "Oh
my God," Arnie said to the Englishman. "You finished
terrible, didn't you," and Westwood nodded. Arnie
continued: "And then you walked up the hill and shook
my hand with a big smile on your face. If that had been
me, I'd have been chewing the f***ing grass."

Arnie had the ability to put a smile on the face of most
people. It was one of his gifts.

Greg Norman

April blues

Greg Norman once described Augusta National as "a cruel temptress". He had more than his fair share of heartbreak at the Masters, witnessing Larry Mize deny him a green jacket in 1987 with an outrageous chip-in at the second playoff hole, and then in 1993 having his six-stroke overnight lead whittled away by Nick Faldo, who ended up winning by five.

Greg had another golden opportunity to win in 1986. As Jack Nicklaus charged through the field on the back nine on Sunday, it's often overlooked that Greg, who led by one after 54 holes, was tied for the lead on the final hole, having made four successive birdies from the 14th, which included a remarkable shot between two trees to the left of the 17th fairway.

He hit a perfect 3-wood down the centre of the 18th, leaving himself 187 yards to the pin. It was then that he made what he said later was his "biggest regret in golf". He chose to finesse a 4-iron into the green, rather than hit a hard 5-iron. As soon as it left the clubface, he hung his head in disappointment. The ball sailed into the crowd to the right of the green and an inevitable bogey followed. "If I could have one career mulligan, I'd take it there," he said later.

Nicklaus ended up winning his sixth green jacket, although later that year Greg won his first Open Championship at Turnberry.

Ben Hogan

The greatest comeback

Of Ben Hogan's nine major titles, the most remarkable
is surely the 1950 US Open at Merion. On 2 February
the previous year, driving home from a tournament in
Phoenix, Ben was involved in a sickening head-on crash
with a Greyhound bus that left him with a double fracture
of the pelvis, a fractured collar bone and left ankle, and
a cracked rib. A blood clot problem meant doctors had to
tie off the largest vein in his body, the vena cava, leaving
him with lifelong circulation problems. It was thought he
might never walk again, much less play golf.

By the time of the US Open in June he was fully
competitive again. Before teeing up, he soaked his body
in a hot bath with Epsom Salts for an hour and then
wrapped his legs in bandages to reduce the swelling.

At halfway, he was two back. How would his body
cope playing 36 holes on the final day?

He shot 72 in the morning round, and then on the 18th
in the final round, needing a par to make a playoff, he
hit one of the great shots in major championship history
which was later commemorated with a plaque in the
fairway. A 1-iron from over 200 yards found the green,
from where he two-putted.

The next day, a 69 in the playoff against Lloyd Mangrum
and George Fazio won Ben his second US Open.

Sandy Lyle

Born 1958

Second-hand driver

A few weeks before the Open Championship at Royal St George's in 1985, Sandy Lyle was horribly out of form. In windy conditions in the first round of the Irish Open at Royal Dublin, he shanked his second shot on the 18th out of bounds and walked in, sparing himself the embarrassment of signing for a score north of 90.

To cure his driving woes, he picked up a new driver, a MacGregor Keyhole. It had belonged to Eamonn Darcy, but he didn't like it and passed it on to Ian Woosnam, who also rejected it. "I can't use this thing," he told Sandy. "Do you want it?" Sandy had always loved MacGregor clubs and after putting a new Pro-Pel steel shaft in it took it with him to Sandwich.

Driving was the key to Sandy's victory at the Open that year. On the last day, the drive at the 15th was played into a stiff wind with a very narrow landing area. Sandy hit his best drive of the week. His playing partner Christy O'Connor Jr needed a 4-wood for his second shot; Sandy played a 6-iron. He hit it to 20 feet and made the birdie.

His new driver never worked for him again. Sandy called it a one-week wonder. But it had done its job. The head of the driver is now on a plinth in a trophy cabinet in Sandy's house.

Severiano Ballesteros

Easy Ryder

One event, more than any other, motivated Seve Ballesteros: the Ryder Cup. As a player and then as captain, he was desperate to beat the Americans. This desire to win brought out a side of Seve that didn't endear him to his opponents.

At the 1987 Ryder Cup at Muirfield Village, Ohio, he and compatriot José María Olazábal played a fourball match on the first day against Curtis Strange and Tom Kite. On the 1st, Olazábal ran a birdie attempt past the hole and was about to putt out when Strange stopped him, arguing that he would be stepping on his through-line. Seve said to Strange, "That bother you?" And the American said, "Yes, it bothers me."

So, Seve marched back to his ball, which was just off the green. Having conversed with Olazábal to this point in Spanish, he said in English, loud enough for his opponents to hear, "Don't worry, this is an easy chip. I'm going to hole it." Which he did. He picked his ball out of the hole and as he walked off the green, pumping his fist, he said to Strange, "Any problem with the through-line now?"

Then he said to Olazábal, "Curtis isn't going to hole his putt." And again, Seve was right. Strange said later he didn't know whether to applaud Seve or kill him. The Spanish pairing went on to win the match 2&1.

Tiger Woods

One-legged Open

Steve Williams caddied for Tiger Woods for 12 years from 1999, during which time one of Tiger's most remarkable major championship victories came at the US Open in 2008.

After finishing second in the Masters that year, Tiger underwent arthroscopic surgery to trim a damaged cartilage in his left knee. Between the operation and the US Open in June, he played no competitive golf. The Sunday before the championship he practised in a knee brace and shot 53 for nine holes, losing eight balls. He ditched the knee brace.

He kept secret that he had ruptured his ACL the previous July and by the time he played at Torrey Pines he was also suffering from two stress fractures of the left tibia.

He opened with a one-over-par 72, four shots off the lead, and on the first hole of his second round hit a wild tee shot onto a cart path. He could have taken a drop but chose to play the ball where it lay.

Williams remembers at impact there was a horrible sound, like his leg had broken, and he could see Tiger was in great pain. He told Tiger that perhaps now would be a good time to quit. Tiger looked at him and said, "F**k you, I'm winning this tournament."

Which he did, beating Rocco Mediate in a 19-hole playoff. Tiger played 91 holes, pretty much on one leg, and wincing in pain after almost every shot.

Darren Clarke

Born 1968

Over-celebrating

If there was one thing that eclipsed Darren Clarke's Open Championship victory at Royal St George's in 2011 then it was the obligatory press conference he gave the next morning. "I take credit for the fact that no Open champion has held a similar press conference since," Darren said. "[R&A chief executive] Martin Slumbers told me I killed it."

For the record, a 42-year-old Darren won the 140th Open by three shots, and as many champions have done before and since, he and his friends celebrated in his rented house. And they celebrated. And they celebrated. And then they celebrated some more.

The next morning a dishevelled, and clearly still inebriated Open champion returned to Royal St George's. He was asked how many hours sleep he got. "Zero," he said. "I've not been to bed yet. It's ten past nine, probably won't get to bed until some time tomorrow." He was then asked how he celebrated. Slurring his words, Darren said, "Quite a few pints, quite a few beers, quite a few glasses of red wine, and it all continued until about..." – he paused to look at his watch – "30 minutes ago."

He went on to say that he had received 294 congratulatory emails, "but the writing is far too small for me to look at them at this stage. I will look at them tomorrow and try and figure them out."

Jack Nicklaus

Shooting from the hip

Jack Nicklaus won the first of his six Masters titles in 1963, but he admits that an injury helped him into the green jacket that year.

Earlier in the season, during an event in San Francisco, he played an 8-iron into a green and felt pain in his left hip. It got worse overnight, and the next day he missed his first PGA Tour cut.

He was told by a doctor that it was tendonitis and was given a series of cortisone shots before heading straight back out on the road – to Palm Springs, to play in the Bob Hope Classic. Although the pain had eased, he found he couldn't play with his customary power fade. He was forced to clear his problem hip out of the way through impact and play with an unfamiliar draw. He took to it well. He won the tournament.

Over the course of the next ten weeks, Jack had a total of 25 injections in his hip, and by the time he arrived at Augusta his hip was fine. Had he chosen to, he could have reverted to his signature fade, but as he had discovered from his four previous appearances at the Masters, Augusta predominately favours players that hit from right to left.

Jack's hip injury had serendipitously given him the confidence to play with a draw and he won the Masters by one shot from Tony Lema.

"Success depends almost entirely on how effectively you learn to manage the game's two ultimate adversaries: the course and yourself."

Jack Nicklaus

Tom Kite

Born 1949

High as a Kite

In June 1980, Tom Kite put a club in his bag that helped change the game. Up to that point, pros carried wedges with only 56 degrees of loft, but Tom was the first to go with a 60-degree wedge, otherwise known as an L-wedge or lob wedge. Now everyone carries one. It changed Tom's fortunes. In 1981, he was the leading money winner on tour.

His most famous shot with his L-wedge came at Pebble Beach, California, in the final round of the 1992 US Open. By now, a 42-year-old Tom had won more money on the PGA Tour than any other player in history, but he had never won a major. Many thought he just couldn't handle the pressure.

He was level with Gil Morgan at three under when he stood on the tee at the short 7th. The wind was so strong he said none of the 14 clubs he had in his bag was the right club. He selected his 6-iron to hit the ball 107 yards and pulled it into the rough.

It drew a good lie and taking his L-wedge he threw the ball up into the wind. The ball landed about 40 feet short of the pin on the fast sloping green. If it hadn't dropped into the hole it would have run about 20 feet past.

He played the next ten holes in just one over par to win his one and only major championship by two shots.

Phil Mickelson

Sneaky Phil

Phil Mickelson rarely plays a game of golf unless a bet is involved, and the thought of winning a few bucks drives him to great lengths to make sure he wins. One day, he played a big money game with fellow pros Ben Crane and Colt Knost at Madison Club, in La Quinta, California. Making up the four was an anonymous TV writer who was given as many as 24 strokes over the 18 holes.

Phil insisted on playing with Crane, and they reluctantly allowed the TV writer to play off the forward tees because he couldn't drive the ball more than about 200 yards. On the 1st tee, the writer had a 30-yard advantage, but when they got to the 2nd hole, the gap between the tee boxes was not as far. By the time they got to about halfway through the front nine they found that the gap between tee boxes was reduced even further.

It was then that Knost realized what had happened. Phil had called the pro shop and asked them to shorten the distance between the tee boxes, thereby reducing the advantage Knost and his partner thought they would be getting.

"The son-of-a-bitch," Knost said afterwards – although he admitted it was an impressive play by Phil.

Jon Rahm

Born 1994

Stick to the routine

When Jack Nicklaus offers advice on how to tackle major championships, it's wise to listen. Jack once told Jon Rahm that his pre-major routine had always been to practise at the major venue the previous week, then fly home and put his clubs away until it was time to return and play the championship. Before the Masters in 2023, Jon followed Jack's lead – with one crucial difference.

After three intense days of practice at Augusta, Jon flew home to Arizona to play in a skins game with some friends at his home club, Silverleaf, in Scottsdale. He told his wife Kelley, "We're going to have some fun." They brought music out onto the course, a few cigars, and some booze. In fact, a *lot* of booze. Jon hit driver on every hole that wasn't a par-3 and began with a drive and a wedge for an eagle at the 1st. As the holes went by his alcohol consumption increased and by the 8th things had started to get a little hazy.

Only when they had finished, and the scores added up, did Jon discover he had shot 60. He flew back to Augusta on the Monday, as Jack would have done, and won the Masters – something Jack also did quite frequently.

Jon was asked if 60 was his record score at Silverleaf, and he said he had shot 59 twice – but both times he was sober.

Annika Sörenstam

When Annika threw a tournament

You might think professional golfers are born with such an innate competitive instinct that they will stop at nothing in the pursuit of victory.

It wasn't that way with Annika Sörenstam. As a schoolgirl, she was so shy she would do anything to avoid the limelight. In class, she wouldn't put her hand up to answer a question for fear of getting it wrong and looking a fool.

That shyness extended to the golf course. In a school event, Annika admitted to deliberately missing a putt to avoid having to give a winner's speech. And another time she remembers purposely leaving a shot in the bunker for the same reason.

Public speaking was always her greatest fear. She says she once finished second in a tournament and although she was trying to win, the silver lining was that she wouldn't have to make a speech. Or so she thought. All the competitors were asked to say something, and she stood there thinking, I might as well have won.

Over the years, she's become more comfortable speaking in public. To help face down her demons, at the ANA Inspiration one year – now the Chevron Championship – she wrote "Face Your Fears" under the brim of her visor.

Johnny Miller

Putting blues

In 1997, Johnny Miller took on Jack Nicklaus in a special TV match recorded for the popular series *Shell's Wonderful World of Golf*. Johnny said he had been looking forward to playing the match for a long time because he was facing his hero on a course he loved, The Olympic Club, in San Francisco.

Johnny admitted that putting was his Achilles' heel. His greatest rounds were driven by his exceptional iron play and on this day, in front of the Shell TV cameras, he said his putting "short-circuited". He three-putted seven times, and later had cause to thank the show's editors because they omitted five of them. From tee to green, he matched Jack, but on the greens he said he choked. "It was like I was holding a snake in my hands," he said afterwards. "I couldn't make a three-footer. There is no worse feeling than standing over a short putt, knowing you've got no chance to make it."

Nicklaus shot a 70 to Miller's 81 and afterwards said tactfully, "It was one of those days when one guy just didn't get it going."

Sam Snead

A matter of inches

Golf is littered with stories of players who have been denied victory in major championships by the slimmest of margins. In the case of Sam Snead at the 1947 US Open the margin was just 30 inches.

Going into the final round at St Louis Country Club, Missouri, Sam and Bobby Locke were one shot behind the little-known Virginian Lew Worsham.

Worsham closed with a 71, and while Locke fell away with a 73, Sam holed a birdie putt on the last to take the championship into an 18-hole playoff. Given he had two majors under his belt and over 40 tour wins, compared to Worsham's one tour victory, Sam was a hot favourite.

They came to the final hole all square. Up on the green, Worsham's downhill chip from the apron lipped out, leaving him 30 inches away. Sam had a 15-foot birdie putt to win but left it the same distance short. He was about to hole out when Worsham, in an act of gamesmanship, interrupted him and waved in the officials with a tape measure to determine who was furthest away. It took several minutes before it was decided what Sam already knew – he was about half an inch outside Worsham's ball. Flustered by the interruption, he missed his putt, leaving Worsham with an easy putt to win the US Open.

Sam never won his national Open.

Pádraig Harrington

Born 1971

The unbeliever

The only time Pádraig Harrington felt embarrassed on a golf course was playing the 72nd hole at Carnoustie in the 2007 Open. He held a one-shot lead and after driving into the Barry Burn, hit his next shot, a 4-iron, about 150 yards into the same hazard. Pádraig said, "If they could have subbed me off, I'd have said, 'thank you very much'." His caddie (and brother-in-law) Ronan Flood tried to settle his man, telling him it wasn't over, finish the hole and see where you are, all the usual cliches. "I wanted to kill him," Pádraig said. "Ronan had to take the club off me because I would have hit him." Friends of his at home turned off their TVs at this point. Someone even broke theirs. "These are the people I was dying with," Pádraig said.

As they walked down the fairway, Pádraig was silent. Ronan was saying to him, "Come on, you hear me," and eventually Pádraig said, "Yes, OK, yes." Pádraig gathered his composure to hit a superb chip to five feet and then holed the putt to tie Sergio García. A little later, Pádraig won the four-hole playoff for his first Open title.

He says that Ronan won him that Open because he didn't let his head slump. Afterwards, Pádraig said to him, "You kept believing, didn't you," to which Ronan replied, "No, I thought you'd lost the f***ing Open as well."

Justin Leonard

Born 1972

The gatecrasher

In 1999, at Brookline, Massachusetts, Justin Leonard
sank one of the most famous putts in the history of the
Ryder Cup – famous not only for its brilliance, helping
the Americans regain the cup, but for the scenes of
pandemonium it provoked from teammates. As Justin
ran wide-eyed in celebration around the green, the first
person to envelop him in a congratulatory hug was a
man in a red shirt. It wasn't a player, or even a member
of the American back room staff. In fact, Mike Hoey
wasn't even supposed to be there. And yet, there he was,
inside the ropes, standing by a bunker at the 17th hole.

Mike had forged a ticket and written CLERGY on
it, and that week posed as the official chaplain of the
American team. For a year or more, Justin believed
he was genuinely a man of the cloth, until someone
enlightened him. Mike Hoey was a bricklayer from
Boston, who made a career out of crashing America's
greatest sporting events. In 1985, he ended up in
the Boston Celtics locker room after they beat the
LA Lakers in an NBA finals game.

"I can't imagine the nerves on that guy," Justin said
many years later. "He's become part of the story. The
quirkiness of Brookline, and the incredible history of
the Ryder Cup. He just fits for some reason. He's
oddly appropriate."

"You must work very hard to become a natural golfer."

Gary Player

Gary Player

Down in the dunes

In 1955, Gary Player left his home in South Africa for the first time, with £200 in his pocket that his father had had to take out an overdraft to give him, and a £125 plane ticket paid for by the members of his club in Johannesburg. His destination was St Andrews, and the 84th Open Championship.

He said when he arrived at Leuchars station he was completely lost and given a lift to the course by British player John Jacobs. The first night he couldn't find a hotel room he could afford, so he donned his waterproofs and slept in the dunes overlooking West Sands Beach, the setting for the movie *Chariots of Fire.*

He played the Old Course the next day in the first round of qualifying. He was so nervous his opening drive hit a fence post. He said the starter laughed at him and asked what his handicap was. Gary told him he was a pro. "A pro!" the starter said. "You must be a hell of a good chipper and putter because you cannae hit the ball very well, laddie."

Gary failed to make it through qualifying, but at Muirfield four years later, in 1959, he won the first of his three Opens. The following year he returned to St Andrews as defending champion. This time he was able to afford quite a nice hotel room and didn't have to sleep in the dunes.

Paul Azinger

Born 1960

SEALing the Ryder Cup

Lying on his sofa in his living room and watching a documentary on the Discovery Channel about Navy SEALs gave Paul Azinger an idea that helped his American team win the Ryder Cup in 2008. Team USA had lost the previous two matches by a combined score of 37-19. What could captain Zinger do different at Valhalla, Kentucky, to reverse his team's fortunes?

He watched how the SEALs were broken into small groups which ate, slept and trained together. "They bond with each other in a way you can't understand," Zinger said. When it came to the heat of battle, they were more likely to lay everything on the line for a small group of men than for the whole battalion. "It was the key to military success," he said. "At that moment, I thought it could be the key to America's Ryder Cup woes as well."

He thought the different nationalities of players on the European team created ready-made pods. He emulated the approach of the Navy SEALs, but with one important variation. He created three pods of three players, each one with an assistant captain, and then left it to pod members to select a fourth player from a shortlist of captain's picks – a player whose personality was compatible with those in the pod. Zinger said it helped get his team engaged in the match a month before it had even started.

USA won the Ryder Cup 16½-11½.

Bernhard Langer

Born 1957

A tale of two putts

It's been called the most high-pressure putt in the history of the Ryder Cup. The permutations were simple: if Bernhard Langer holed from six feet on the 18th green at Kiawah Island, South Carolina, in 1991, he would win his singles match against Hale Irwin and Europe would retain the Ryder Cup. Miss, and victory would be America's for the first time since 1983.

Bernhard read the putt as left edge, but there were two half-inch spike marks on his line, about ten inches in front of his ball. He consulted his caddie Peter Coleman, and they agreed it was too risky to hit the putt over the marks. "It definitely would have deflected my ball if I'd hit them," Bernhard said. He decided to avoid them and take the borrow out by hitting the putt straight and firm. He struck what he thought was a perfect putt, but it broke fractionally to the right, brushed the lip, and slid past.

Bernhard had little time to dwell on his misfortune. He was hosting the German Masters in Stuttgart the following week. And as fate would have it, he faced a putt, of about 15 feet this time, on the 72nd green to force a playoff. As he was lining it up, thoughts flooded back from the previous week. "No, don't think about that," he told himself. He made the putt and went on to win the playoff.

Bobby Jones

Calamity Jane

"It was rusty and sort of beat up, and no doubt had several owners before it ever got to me," Bobby Jones said of his putter, arguably the most famous golf club in the world.

The putter was made in London and taken to America by the Scot Jim Maiden, whose brother Stewart was Bobby's coach. After Bobby had been beaten by Francis Ouimet in the US Amateur in 1920 Jim offered it to him. It was 33 inches long, weighed about 15 pounds and had eight degrees of loft. Its hickory shaft was held together with glue and strips of black linen thread.

Jim called it Calamity Jane, but it proved to be anything but calamitous. Bobby won his first three majors with it – the US Open in 1923 and the US Amateur in 1924 and 1925. A clubmaker, J. Victor East, noticing that its face had become worn, made six replicas of the putter, with "Calamity Jane" seared into the back of the blade. One went into Jones' bag, and he used it to win his next ten majors. Six years after his retirement Bobby used the original Calamity Jane in a practice round before the 1936 Masters. He shot 64, taking only 25 putts, and said it was "just like an old friend".

That original putter is in a trophy case at Augusta National, while Calamity Jane Mk II is in the USGA's museum in New Jersey.

Nick Price

Born 1957

One hand on the trophy

Nick Price won the Open Championship at Turnberry in 1994, but 12 years earlier, at Royal Troon, he made the mistake of thinking he had the job done, only for the Claret Jug to slip through his grasp.

Price started the last day two shots ahead of Tom Watson, but when he looked at the leaderboard walking off the 9th green he saw he was now two behind. He said to his caddie Kevin Woodward, "If we're going to win this, we have to make some birdies." And that's what he did: three successive birdies from the 10th, and a Watson bogey, meant Nick had a two-shot lead with six to play. Walking onto the 13th tee, he said to his caddie, "That's it. We're going to win this thing now."

Nick said he never made such a foolhardy comment in his career again. He bogeyed the 13th, and a bad bounce in front of the green at the 14th took his approach shot into a pot bunker. He chipped out sideways, and a few minutes later he walked off the green with a double bogey. Another bogey at the 17th meant he lost the Open by a stroke. Afterwards, Watson said, "I didn't win the championship, Price lost it."

It taught Nick two things: one, not to count his chickens, but also that he had the game that was good enough to win an Open one day.

Lee Trevino

A record wrapped in clover

During the week of the 1968 US Open at Oak Hill, in Rochester, Lee Trevino stayed with a local family, the Kirchers, who had seven children. The youngest daughter, Susan, was just two, and one day she and Lee went out onto the back lawn and lay on the grass searching for four-leaf clovers. Lee found one and kept it in his back pocket the whole week.

Lee had a big lead standing on the 18th tee in the final round, so victory was all but guaranteed, but his goal was to par the last and become the first man to shoot four rounds in the 60s in a US Open. He pulled his drive into the left hand rough and his caddie, a college student called Kevin Quinn, advised him to take a wedge and lay up in front of the green. Lee replied, "No, I don't want to be remembered as the guy that wins the US Open laying up. I don't lay up. Give me the 6-iron."

Lee advanced the ball no more than 50 yards and left it in the rough. He struck his next shot, with a wedge, to about four feet and then a few minutes later holed the putt for a closing round of 69.

"My God, he looks like he's beating a chicken."

Byron Nelson

Nelly Korda

Born 1998

Villain of the piece

At the 2021 Solheim Cup at Inverness, in Toledo, Nelly Korda was unwittingly cast as the villain in a rules controversy. She was playing with her American partner Ally Ewing in a first day fourballs match against the European pair of Nanna Koerstz Madsen and Madelene Sagström.

At the 13th, with the match all square, Nelly left a 30-foot eagle putt on the edge of the hole. The Europeans conceded the putt and Sagström picked the ball up and tossed it back to Nelly. The rule states that if a ball is hanging over the lip of a hole a player can wait ten seconds to see if it will drop. Apparently, Sagström picked the ball up after only seven seconds. Nelly's putt was recorded as an eagle and America won the hole, even though Europe insisted the ball was not hanging over the lip – and certainly television pictures seemed to back that up. Nelly received a lot of criticism for accepting the ruling, but she didn't have any option. In golf, rules are absolute.

Later, Nelly holed a vital putt of similar length at the 18th for a par, and when Sagström missed a birdie putt from about 25 feet, America had won the match, 1 up. Nelly said afterwards, "It was definitely awkward, you don't want to win a hole like that." However, the incident didn't dent Europe's confidence. They won the Solheim Cup 15-13.

Byron Nelson

1912–2006

The Iron Byron

In 1945, Byron Nelson set a record that will probably never be matched. He won 11 tournaments in a row, over a period of five months and three days, and won 18 times during the season.

Jack Nicklaus said he was the straightest hitter of a golf ball he had ever seen. Members of Glen Garden Golf Club, in Fort Worth, where Byron played, claimed he could hit dozens of balls 200 yards and you could throw a blanket over all of them. Byron's mantra was: "Swing the club as though you were driving 60 miles an hour on the highway. Not too fast, but not deathly slow."

In 1963, golf manufacturer True Temper commissioned engineer George Manning to build a robotic machine to demonstrate the most efficient, repeatable swing. Manning examined photographs of all the top players' swings, and one, above all others, stood out. He said later, "We were looking to have a very efficient swing – and what I mean by efficient is a minimum amount of energy for a maximum distance hit. We discovered Byron Nelson had an extremely repeatable and efficient swing. So, we designed the machine to copy that swing." The machine was called Iron Byron.

Initially, Iron Byron was used by the USGA to test clubs and balls, to ensure they conformed to industry standards. But gradually it was used as a teaching device, with pupils encouraged to imitate the machine's swing.

Jim Furyk

Furyk's faux pas

In his first event as a rookie on the PGA Tour in 1994, Jim Furyk was warming up on the range. It was early morning, with a right-to-left wind blowing strongly into the players' faces. Jim was at the far right edge of the range and turned 45 degrees to hit a wedge to a flag about 50 yards away. It was early morning and the range was wet and very sandy. He hit the shot about three inches fat and a huge spray of sand coated the player warming up next to him. Jim turned and said, "Sorry about that," and discovered to his horror it was Lanny Wadkins. "That's about as intimidating as it can get," Jim said later. He then looked at his father and pulled a face, as if to say, Holy crap, what have I just done?

He scraped another ball over and took aim at the same pin. As he was over the ball he realized he was now feeling quite nervous. And again, he hit the ball fat and this time he could *hear* the sand hitting Wadkins. After another apology, Jim said, "I guess I'll aim a little further right."

Lanny was over his shot and without even breaking stride, looked up at Jim and said, "That'd be nice."

Ian Woosnam

Born 1958

Back to good form

For much of 1986, Ian Woosnam struggled with a bad back. At the end of the year, he went to a specialist who told him he had ankylosing spondylitis, a form of spinal arthritis. The doctor said there was good news and bad news, so Woosie asked for the good news first. "You might be able to play for another ten years," the doctor said.

"And the bad news?"

"In ten years' time, you could be in a wheelchair."

He was put on a regimen of anti-inflammatories and Woosie felt instant relief. At last, he could sleep without having to put a suitcase under his mattress and swing a golf club pain free. At New Year's Eve, he had a party at his house in Oswestry, and a friend suggested that at the stroke of midnight he went outside and hit a golf ball into 1987. Despite wearing what he called his "dancing shoes" he did just that, noticing in the process that he was able to stay more on his right side, something his bad back had prevented him from doing and which meant Woosie was often fighting a hook.

He took that swing thought with him on tour in 1987, and enjoyed the most prolific season in his career, winning nine times around the world, and finishing as leader of the Order of Merit.

Fred Couples

Born 1959

Freddie's missing 7-iron

Fred Couples was standing over his ball on the 18th fairway in the final round of the 1992 Buick Classic at Westchester Country Club, New York, considering what club he needed for his second shot. On the bag that day was Joe LaCava, who caddied for Freddie for over 20 years. LaCava told his man he had 205 yards to the pin. Freddie said he liked a 6-iron, but LaCava disagreed. "A seven," he said. "But I like six," Freddie said. "I like seven," the caddie reiterated.

Freddie went with the seven. Hit it well. "Pounded on it," he recalled. It finished short of the green. In disgust, he threw the 7-iron at LaCava's feet and marched up to the green, where he chipped and two-putted for a par.

Freddie and his caddie then hopped on a plane and flew to Pebble Beach, California, for a tournament the following week. On the range on the Tuesday, Freddie went through his clubs, only to find that the 7-iron was missing.

"Joe, where's my seven?" he asked.

"Where you left it," came the reply. Freddie's 7-iron – the club belonging to the reigning Masters champion and the then world number one – was back on the 18th fairway at Westchester.

Freddie lost it, but then when he calmed down, he said he laughed about it. In 2022, Freddie hired LaCava's son, Joe Jr, to caddie for him on the Champions Tour.

Geoff Ogilvy

Born 1977

Mum knows best

One year, when Geoff Ogilvy was playing in what is now called the Genesis Invitational at Riviera Country Club, in Los Angeles, his caddie Alistair "Squirrel" Matheson answered a telephone call on a tee box.

Today, the 10th at Riviera is a driveable par-4, and most players take their driver and go for the green, but when Geoff was on tour it was played more conventionally – a long iron to short of the fairway bunker and a wedge to the green. Infuriated by a double bogey at the 9th, Geoff walked onto the 10th tee and asked Squirrel for his driver.

"It's a 3-iron over there," Squirrel said, pointing to the lay-up area.

"No, I'm hitting driver," Geoff said.

"Well, you're wrong," Squirrel reiterated. "It's a 3-iron over there."

"Get out of the way," Geoff said. "I'm hitting driver."

Geoff hit driver – and ended up making double bogey. On the 11th tee, as Geoff was over the ball, Squirrel's phone rang. He quietly unzipped the bag and answered it. After a few seconds Squirrel said to the caller, "Sorry, I'm on the course," and hung up. Geoff turned to his caddie and said, "What are you doing answering the phone in the middle of a golf tournament? And who was that anyway?"

"That was my mum," Squirrel said. "She said no one hits driver on the 10th at Riviera."

Walter Hagen

Where's the cup?

In 1925, the Haig won – and lost – the Wanamaker Trophy. He had just claimed his third USPGA title – at Olympia Fields, Chicago – and, like many champions before and since, went off to celebrate, taking the trophy with him. Before slipping into a nightclub, Walter paid a cab driver $5 to return the giant piece of silverware to his hotel.

It was the last he ever saw of it.

He arrived at Salisbury Golf Links, New York, 12 months later without the Wanamaker Trophy. When asked where it was, he said he hadn't brought it because he was going to successfully defend his title, and therefore wouldn't have to relinquish it.

He kept his word, defeating Leo Diegel 5&3 in the final. And he won again, for the fourth time in a row, in 1927 at Cedar Crest Country Club, in Dallas. Only after an early exit in 1928 – at the hands of eventual champion Diegel – did he finally 'fess up. The PGA had to make a replacement Wanamaker Trophy. Three years later, the original was found in the basement of L.A. Young & Company, a firm which produced Walter Hagen golf clubs.

"You're only here for a short visit. Don't hurry, don't worry. And be sure to smell the flowers along the way."

Walter Hagen

Luke Donald

Born 1977

Prize beef

For successful tour pros, golf can be a cash cow. Literally, in the case of Luke Donald.

When Luke won the Dunlop Phoenix tournament in Japan in 2012, his first prize cheque came with another reward – a cow. Taking an animal home on an aeroplane to his home in Chicago was clearly not going to be possible, so Luke, a self-confessed foodie, contacted a chef he knew, who in turn arranged for the meat from the prized Miyazaki cow to be imported.

It then transpired that the cow was still alive, and so Luke was asked which cuts he wanted, and how many pounds of each he was after. In the end, it was agreed that Luke would receive 200 pounds of Miyazaki beef, one of the world's most coveted meats and which, at the time, top restaurants paid about $160 a pound for.

Eventually, a meat importer received the meat at his warehouse, cut it up into individual portions and froze it until Luke was ready to collect it. In May the following year, a few months after his victory, the golfer took about $80,000 worth of beef home with him, and immediately threw some onto the grill.

"It's very marbled and the knife just eases through the meat," Luke said. "Definitely the best beef I've ever had."

Tom Watson

The duel in the sun

Tom Watson's very first shot on a links course was in
July 1975 at Monifieth Golf Club, a few days before the
Open at nearby Carnoustie. He was playing a practice
round and his opening drive split the fairway – only for
the ball to shoot sideways and disappear into the rough.
"I don't know if I'm gonna like this," Tom said. It's safe
to say he quickly learned to love links golf. He not only
won the Open that year, but did so again in 1977, 1980,
1982 and 1983.

His most memorable victory was at Turnberry in 1977,
the so-called Duel in the Sun, when he and Jack Nicklaus
went head-to-head in the final round.

They were level heading to the 16th tee on the final
day when Tom turned to his rival and said, "This is what
it's all about, isn't it?" "You bet it is," came the reply. At
the 17th, Nicklaus fell one behind Tom, who then all
but sealed the win with a 7-iron shot to two feet at the
final hole. With Nicklaus 35 feet away, Alfie Fyles, Tom's
caddie, said to his man, "Well, sir, you got him now,"
but Tom knew better. "No, I don't," he replied. "We have
to expect him to make this putt." And sure enough,
Nicklaus did, leaving Tom with his little putt to clinch
the title.

Vijay Singh

Born 1963

Ball skimming

Vijay Singh may have hit the greatest shot in the history of the Masters. The reason it's not better known is because it occurred during a practice round. It's become a Masters tradition that at Augusta National's short 16th players throw a ball down on the edge of the giant pond in front of the tee and try and skim the ball over the water and onto the green. The crowd loves it.

In 2009, Vijay, without so much as a practice swing, skimmed the ball about six times across the lake and onto the green. It then began to slowly curve down towards the pin. A few feet short of the hole the crowd began to sense something extraordinary might be about to happen. And, sure enough, the ball dropped dead weight into the hole for the unlikeliest ace. Vijay, never one to show much emotion at the best of times, simply strode off towards the green, as though it was something he did every day of the week.

Lee Trevino claims to have started the tradition in the late 1980s. One Masters Sunday, when he was well out of contention in the tournament, he said the pond was "beautiful, like glass". He skimmed the ball onto the green and a few minutes later walked off it having two-putted for a par. "Anything anti-establishment, I started," he said.

Mark O'Meara

Born 1957

Tiger envy

When Tiger Woods moved to Isleworth, Florida, four doors down from Mark O'Meara, the pair became great friends. Throughout his career, Tiger used a Scotty Cameron Newport 2 GSS putter, winning all but one of his major titles with it, but apparently he coveted the Ping Anser 2 putter Mark used.

Mark wouldn't let Tiger use it in competition. Even so, Tiger begged Mark that he leave it to him in his will. However, for a few months in 1998, he did lend Tiger his spare Anser 2, and he used it to great effect in the Open that year at Royal Birkdale, finishing a stroke behind the eventual champion – one Mark O'Meara!

On the flight home, clutching the Claret Jug, Mark teased Tiger. "You know why it's my backup putter?" he asked. "Because it always comes up one shot shy." Tiger said he was never going to use that putter again.

One day, Rickie Fowler was over at Mark's house and took a picture of himself with the Anser 2 putter on Mark's putting green. He then sent the picture to Tiger, who, according to Mark, responded immediately. "What the hell are you doing putting with my putter?" the text read. "That is not your putter. M.O. is going to leave that putter for me and don't be putting with my putter."

Mark said he had no intention of bequeathing the putter to Tiger.

Patty Berg

1918–2006

One of the greats

In 1942, Patty Berg volunteered for the US Marine Corps. At 24, she had already won three Titleholders Championships, an event that was later designated a major by the LPGA and was one of the best players in the world. But she had had a car accident the previous year, shattering her knee, and she wondered if she would ever play at the highest level again. Patty was a great patriot. Fellow LPGA Hall of Famer Betsy King remembers she would conclude her golf clinics with the words, "God bless you. And God bless America."

First Lieutenant Patricia Berg served as an officer in the Eastern Procurement Division in Philadelphia until the end of World War II. Her job was to go around college campuses in the country and recruit officers who were fit, ready and willing to serve their country in battle. LPGA historian Steve Eubanks describes Berg as the "consummate salesperson" and a "close-the-deal dynamo". She later became the first woman to be inducted into the United States Marine Corps Sports Hall of Fame.

Although she never recovered full movement in her knee, Patty returned to competitive golf, winning another 12 major championships, including the inaugural US Women's Open in 1946. Her total of 15 majors remains the all-time record for a woman golfer. In 1950, she became a founder member of the LPGA, later serving as its first President.

Corey Pavin

Born 1959

Presidential Pavin

The week before his victory in the 1995 US Open at Shinnecock Hills, in Long Island, Corey Pavin played a round of golf with the sitting US President, Bill Clinton.

After his second round at the Kemper Open, at TPC Avenel, Potomac, just a few miles from the White House, Corey rang Clinton and suggested a round of golf. They had met the previous year and the President told Corey to give him a call when he was in town. They played that afternoon at the Army Navy Country Club, in Arlington. Corey remembers ribbing Clinton about Arkansas being beaten by his alma mater UCLA in the NCAA basketball final.

Despite losing a sudden death playoff to Lee Janzen for the Kemper title, Corey arrived at Shinnecock in buoyant mood, and ended up winning his one and only major title by two shots from Greg Norman.

Later, having done his post-event press conference and spoken to the world's media, Corey was looking forward to going out and celebrating with his friends and family. By now darkness had fallen and as he walked to his courtesy car, he was handed a telephone. "Phone call for you, Corey."

"Take a message," Corey replied. "I'm done."

"I think you might want to take *this* call."

It was President Clinton, who offered his congratulations to his golfing buddy. "I guess all those tips I gave you last week paid off, huh," said the President.

"I play golf with friends sometimes, but there are never friendly games."

Ben Hogan

Jack Nicklaus

Me and Mr Jones

Jack Nicklaus' father Charlie idolized Bobby Jones and it was an admiration that extended to his son. They first met when Jack was 15. He was playing a practice round ahead of the 1955 US Amateur in windy conditions at the Country Club of Virginia, in Richmond. At the 18th, he hit a 3-wood through the wind and onto the green.

A man had been watching from a golf cart and after Jack had holed out, someone said to him, "Mr Jones would like to meet you."

Bobby Jones congratulated Jack on being one of the few players to have reached the green in two that day. In his first-round match, Jack was 1 up at the turn against Bob Gardner. But then Jones appeared on the 10th fairway in his cart and Jack proceeded to go bogey-bogey-double bogey. Jones said to Charlie, "I don't think I'm doing Jack much good. I'm going to get out of here." Jack lost his match, 1 down.

In 1959, Jack qualified for the Masters for the first time and in his locker found a note from Jones, inviting him and his father to the Jones Cabin to say hello. Jack found a similar invitation in his locker every year.

"When he passed, I missed my visit down with him," Jack said. "It was a big empty hole for the week. I learned an awful lot from him. He was my idol."

Severiano Ballesteros

Trapeze artist

The golf writer Bill Elliott was a good friend of Seve
Ballesteros and he was at Augusta when the Spaniard
won his first Masters title in 1980. After the presentation
ceremony, Seve invited the journalist and about 20
friends to a party at his rented house. When he turned
up wearing his new green jacket and grinning from
ear to ear Bill told Seve he had never seen him looking
happier or healthier. Seve's face darkened and he
instructed Bill to follow him to the garage where Seve
had removed the connecting door to the kitchen and
in its place installed a trapeze. "See this," he said. "I
must hang upside down from this for 20 minutes each
morning to try to stretch my back. Every day I have pain.
Healthy? No, not healthy."

He made Bill try it. A few minutes was all he could
stand. Even then, at only 23, Seve suffered from
incessant back pain but he didn't want his opponents
to know in case they saw it as a sign of weakness. As
Bill wrote later, Seve knew his career would not be a
long one.

There has been much debate as to when and how Seve
first experienced back pain. He was a keen boxer as a kid
and one version of events is that he slipped in the ring
during a bout and fell on his coccyx.

Curtis Strange

Born 1955

If you don't win, you lose

"You'll learn." Although, as Curtis Strange acknowledged many years later, he was the one that eventually learned.

On 28 August 1996, on the eve of the Greater Milwaukee Open, Curtis sat down with Tiger Woods for an interview for ABC Sports. Tiger had just turned pro, a few days after winning his third successive US Amateur title, and this was his first professional tournament. It was also Curtis' first sit-down interview and he admitted to being nervous.

Curtis asked the 20-year-old Tiger what he would consider to be a good week. Tiger said to play four solid rounds, and "a victory would be awfully nice, too". Curtis said he was caught off-guard by Tiger's forthright comments. He laughed – some might say, a little patronizingly – and said that in his eyes that came off as a little cocky. Tiger said what's the point playing in tournaments if not to try and win. "Second sucks and third is even worse," he added. Curtis, clearly riled, suggested second or third isn't too bad, but Tiger reiterated his desire to win every time he played. Curtis wished later he had just shut up at this point. Instead, he smiled, looked down at his notes, and said, "You'll learn."

Years later, by which time his "you'll learn" comment had gone viral, Curtis took it back. He admitted to Tiger, "I learned. Maybe I was wrong, and you were right. Or maybe we were both right."

Tiger Woods

A steak in the ground

Joe LaCava succeeded Steve Williams as Tiger Woods' caddie in 2011. He recounts a story of when he first went to dinner with his new employer. Tiger told him to meet at a certain restaurant at 5.30pm and because he wanted to make a good impression LaCava arrived bang on the allotted time. The maître d' told him Tiger was already there, at a table in the back.

In fact, Tiger had already started his meal. He had eaten his salad and was waiting for his steak. LaCava sat down but by the time his salad arrived Tiger had eaten his steak. During their conversation LaCava said Tiger didn't look up from his plate once.

And then, while LaCava was waiting for his main course, Tiger got up and left. LaCava said, "It wasn't in a bad way. But 5.30 for him means 5.15. And if you're not there, he's just going to order."

Apparently, Tiger doesn't even waste time looking at a menu. He knows exactly what he wants, and how he likes it: porterhouse steak, medium rare. With salad.

Greg Norman

Shark bait

Golfers are often heckled by fans during their rounds and most of the time they have learned to tune out the abuse. But Greg Norman let his emotions get the better of him during the final round of the 1986 US Open at Shinnecock Hills, challenging his heckler to a fight. Looking back on it, Greg admits it may have cost him the title.

Greg held a one-shot lead after 54 holes and as he was walking from one of the greens to the next tee, someone from the gallery shouted at him, "Go home you f***ing Aussie...You can't play golf...You're a choker." Greg admits he "kinda lost his cool" and went up to the man and said, "If you want to say something to me, say it to me in the car park at the end of the round when I can do something about it."

Greg knows he broke the sporting code of golf and confesses he should never have done it, saying the incident was "an education" for him to block things out a little better.

Greg played the last ten holes of his final round in four over par and finished five shots behind eventual champion Raymond Floyd.

When asked if his heckler met him in the car park afterwards, Greg replied, "Hell, no."

Ben Hogan

The Iceman cometh

When Ben Hogan arrived at Carnoustie in 1953 for his one and only appearance in the Open Championship, he didn't immediately endear himself to the Scottish public. He complained during his practice rounds that the greens were so slow it was "like putting on glue". He didn't much care for the ragged, sunburned fairways either. He said he had a lawnmower back in Texas and offered to "send it over".

But watching his methodical practice routine – three shots from three different places on every tee – the crowds gradually warmed to him, and they bestowed on him a nickname, The Wee Ice Mon.

And nor was Ben too fond of the weather. Rain and hail accompanied his second round, and when he teed off on the final day, two shots off the lead, he was bundled up in two sweaters, complaining of the flu.

By the time he played the 18th on the final day, three shots clear of his nearest challenger, he had completely won over the Scottish public. Some 20,000 people lined the fairway and encircled the green, a crowd much bigger than anything Ben had experienced in America, and they erupted in joy when he sank his putt for a birdie, putting the gloss on a four-stroke victory.

Mark Calcavecchia

Born 1960

Calc chokes

Johnny Miller said it was the worst shot he had ever seen.

Standing on the 17th tee of his singles match against Colin Montgomerie at Kiawah Island in the 1991 Ryder Cup, Mark Calcavecchia was 2 up with two to play. He had lost two holes on the bounce, but victory seemed assured when Montgomerie hit his tee shot into the water. Monty thought to himself, "I'm finished. That's it. Gone. Done."

Only he wasn't. Calc's shot was even worse. "I smother topped one in the water," he said. On commentary, Roger Maltbie said, "Are you kidding me? It only had about two seconds' hang-time."

A few minutes later, after both players had taken penalty drops, Calc appeared to have been reprieved. Monty missed his long try for bogey, leaving the American with a two-foot putt for the win. Monty was on the verge of conceding. "I was about to go over and shake his hand and say, 'well done'." But he said at the last second "something clicked in me" and he changed his mind.

Calc's putt didn't even threaten the hole. And when Monty won the 18th, the match was halved. Calc was inconsolable. Thinking he had cost his team victory, he went to the beach and cried. When he started hyperventilating a doctor had to be called.

America eventually won the Ryder Cup, by a point. Calc's half was the difference between the two sides.

Phil Mickelson

Heaping on the pressure

At the 2013 Presidents Cup at Muirfield Village, Phil Mickelson was paired with Keegan Bradley in a foursomes match against Graham DeLaet and Jason Day. The Americans were dormie six on their International opponents and seemingly set for a big victory.

On the 13th green, Bradley had a six-foot putt to win the match, but his effort horseshoed out. Bradley walked to the next hole, a par-3, still rattled and carved a 3-iron 100 yards right of the green. DeLaet and Day won the hole, cutting the deficit to four. At the next hole, a par-5, both teams had birdie putts, although DeLaet's was from 25 feet, while Bradley was just five feet from the hole. If DeLaet missed his putt, Team USA would win the point, but to the shock of everybody, not least the players, Phil said to DeLaet, "Pick it up, it's good." Bradley looked at Phil as if to say, "Are you kidding me?" He was angry because now all the pressure was on him. If he missed, their advantage would be just three holes.

Bradley didn't miss, and he and Phil won the match 4&3. As Bradley said afterwards, "He says he knew I was rattled and he wanted me to make that putt to win the match. So, typical Phil, trying to teach lessons. But it was wild. I mean, a 25-footer!"

"The Open
Championship is golf's
greatest stage, where
the drama unfolds
on nature's terms."

Seve Ballesteros

Dai Rees

1913–1983

Duty calls

When Dai Rees enlisted in the Royal Air Force during World War II, his job was as a driver (an appropriate role for a golfer) for Air Marshal Sir Harry Broadhurst, or Broady as he was known, a high-ranking RAF commander. In this role, he also got to meet some of the Allies' top brass, including Field Marshal Bernard Montgomery.

Dai was stationed all over the world, and he was in Holland on 16 December 1944, when Monty, a keen golfer who played the game to relax when he wasn't plotting the Germans' downfall, asked Dai to accompany him to Eindhoven for a round of golf.

According to Dai, they had got as far as the 6th green, with Monty "more than holding his own", when an aide-de-camp rushed out onto the course, looking a little flustered. Apparently, Monty was lining up a tricky eight-footer when the officer said, "The Germans have attacked, sir, at five points along the front in the Ardennes." The attack led to what became known as the Battle of the Bulge.

Monty, channelling his inner Sir Francis Drake, said calmly, "Very well. I'll be along directly." He then holed his putt and left.

After the war, Dai went on to finish second in the Open four times, and in 1957 captained the British and Irish team to Ryder Cup victory at Lindrick.

Arnold Palmer

There in plaque and white

When Arnold Palmer won the first of his two consecutive Open Championships, at Royal Birkdale in 1961, his drive on the 15th in the final round finished in what BBC commentator Henry Longhurst described as "the bottom of a small, sandy bank, buried deep in some blackberry bushes", about 150 yards from the green.

Most players would have chipped out sideways – but, of course, Arnie was not built like other players. He told *The New York Times* later, "I saw the opening. I was sure I would make it. Nobody else was." He took a 6-iron and "never hit the ball so hard in my life". He reached the green and two-putted for a vital par. He went on to win the Claret Jug by one shot from a fast-finishing Dai Rees.

A bronze plaque was laid in the spot to commemorate Arnie's unlikely, and championship-winning shot, and through the years visitors to the course have gone in search of it. Only they won't find it on the 15th anymore; after course reconstruction the plaque now borders the 16th hole.

In 1989, Arnie was playing in the Open at Royal Troon, and at the 11th hole played a recovery shot from the gorse. He asked his caddie Alfie Fyles where the plaque was. "About 200 miles away," the droll Lancastrian replied. Arnie had confused the 15th at Royal Birkdale with the 11th at Royal Troon.

Bryson DeChambeau

Born 1993

Method in the madness

Bryson DeChambeau's nickname is The Mad Scientist, or Sheldon, from the sitcom *The Big Bang Theory*. He admits that 95 per cent of his fellow pros think he's nuts. The physics major has always been fascinated by ball rotation, club path, face angle, "all that fun stuff," he says. He believes adding science to golf can only help.

Since 2011, Bryson has been playing with one-length clubs, which he says gives him the same body posture and swing plane for every shot. At the Masters in 2024, he took eccentricity to a new level. He used something that he had had to print. It wasn't a yardage chart, or a map of the contours of Augusta's notoriously fast greens. It was his clubs – which he had printed on a 3D printer. They had tiny ports in the toe area and some bulge on the face and only got approval from the USGA two days before the Masters started. Bryson said, "It's a speed thing. When I mis-hit on the toe or the heel it flies a lot straighter." He led the Masters after two rounds, eventually finishing tied sixth.

At the Masters in 2016, as an amateur, his irons all had different nicknames branded onto the back of the clubface. Some were named after past champions (Arnie, Jackie) and others after some of Augusta's most famous holes, Azalea and Juniper.

Annika Sörenstam

Mrs 59

Annika Sörenstam remains the only woman to have shot a sub-60 round on the LPGA Tour.

It occurred on 16 March 2001, in the second round of the Standard Register Ping tournament at Moon Valley Country Club, in Phoenix. The portents weren't exactly in her favour when she arrived at the course that morning. She had been held up in traffic and didn't have time to warm up as she would have liked.

It didn't matter. She began at the 10th hole with eight successive birdies, at which point she said she was so nervous she had to make a par at the 18th just to calm herself down. She then carried on the birdie barrage with four successive gains from the 1st. She played the next four holes in one under par, and then in the fairway at the 9th, told her caddie Terry McNamara she was going to play for the flag. She wanted a 58.

She hit her approach to 15 feet but then knocked her birdie putt three feet past. She calmly rolled in the par putt and then leapt into Terry's arms. The crowd around the green erupted.

It hardly needs stating who won the event that week. Annika, of course.

Her playing partners on that day were Meg Mallon and Annika's sister Charlotta, who had won the event the previous year. Mallon shot a one-under-par 71, and said it felt like an 80.

David Duval

Born 1971

Irish nightmare

In the first round of the Open in 2019 at Royal Portrush, in Northern Ireland, the 2001 champion David Duval ran up a 14 on one hole on his way to a 91.

Amazingly, he began the round with two birdies and was briefly on the leaderboard, before losing two balls on the 5th and running up a quadruple bogey. And then things got really bad.

He hit three drives on the par-5 7th – his initial one and two provisionals. A marshal found what they assumed was David's second drive. "I asked if it was a 2 – Titleist 2," David explained. "I looked at it and saw 2 and then played almost the entirety of the hole, and it turns out with the wrong ball." He had to take three two-shot penalties: one, for playing the wrong ball, another for losing his original tee shot, and a third for losing his first provisional ball. He then had to go back to the tee and play his seventh. He hit into the rough, gouged out, and then six shots later, walked off the green with a 14.

There was so much confusion the score initially went down as a 15, before being adjusted to 13, and then finally to 14. "Just one of those God-awful nightmare scenarios that happened today," David said. "And I happened to be on the end of it."

Sam Snead

Bad intel

In 1939, Sam Snead was robbed of an excellent chance to win his national title. With a round to go at Philadelphia Country Club, Craig Wood, Denny Shute and Sam were one shot off the lead. On the final day Sam came to the par-5 18th needing a par to win. In those days, there weren't any leaderboards on the course, and Sam had no idea where he stood in relation to the rest of the field. A spectator told him he needed a birdie to tie Byron Nelson, who had shot a 68. It was duff information; he could have recorded a par and won the title by a stroke.

He pulled his drive into the left rough and thinking he must get on the green in two to make the birdie he needed, he pulled out his 2½-wood and topped it into a bunker. He left his third in the bunker, under the lip, and was unable to advance his fourth shot very far.

His fifth just managed to find the green, from where he three-putted for an eight, finishing two behind Nelson, Wood and Shute. Nelson went on to win the playoff.

In a fax Sam wrote to golf writer Eamon Lynch in 2000, two years before Snead died, he said, "If only I knew the real score, I would have used a 3-iron [for my second shot] and laid up to make an easy five and win."

Thomas Bjørn

Born 1971

Wild card withdraws

In 2018, Thomas Bjørn was the captain of the European Ryder Cup team. Eight golfers played their way onto the team via various points lists, leaving Thomas with four wild card picks of his own.

It appeared life was made harder for Thomas when several months before the match Stephen Atkinson emailed the captain to say that "with a heavy heart" he was making himself ineligible for selection.

Thomas tweeted a response:

Unbelicvable

Where do I go from here?

Stephen, please reconsider @RyderCupEurope

— Thomas Bjørn (@thomasbjorngolf) 23 April 2018

So, who is Stephen Atkinson? And how much of a loss to the team would he be? Well, not very much, since Atkinson was your average club golfer who sent the letter to Thomas as a joke. A few weeks later, Thomas turned up unannounced at Atkinson's house in Berkshire, clutching the Ryder Cup trophy. "This has got way out of hand," an incredulous Atkinson said when he opened his front door.

In the back garden, Atkinson demonstrated his chipping prowess to Thomas. "A bit short, a bit quick," the Dane said. Putting the grand old trophy down on the ground, he proceeded to give Atkinson a golf lesson.

The European team didn't miss Atkinson. They beat the Americans 17½ -10½ in Paris to regain the Ryder Cup.

Lanny Wadkins

Born 1949

Wheelbarrow Wadkins

With 21½ points in 34 matches, Lanny Wadkins is one of the most successful players in the history of the Ryder Cup. Among American players, only Billy Casper and Arnold Palmer have scored more.

In 1983, at PGA National, in Florida, Lanny played one of the greatest Ryder Cup shots, as much for its context as the quality of its execution. In the final day singles, Lanny's match with José María Cañizares was one of only two left on the course. The scores were tied at 13-13, and with Tom Watson beating Bernard Gallacher in the last match, Lanny needed a half to win the cup for his team. He was 3 down to the Spaniard at one point but coming down the par-5 18th he had cut the deficit to just 1 down.

For his third shot, Lanny had 72 yards to the hole and hit his wedge to no more than a foot. Cañizares conceded Lanny's putt and the crucial half point was his. Jack Nicklaus was the American team captain that week. He had never lost a Ryder Cup, and in relief at the preservation of his record, he got down on his hands and knees and kissed the very spot where Lanny had played his pitch shot from. He later gave him the nickname Wheelbarrow, because he said that's what Lanny needed to carry around his huge bollocks.

"Golf is not about
the quality of
your good shots;
it's about the quality
of your bad shots."

Nick Faldo

Bobby Jones

Honest Bob

In the first round the 1925 US Open at Worcester Country Club, Massachusetts, Bobby Jones called a penalty on himself – and he ended up losing the championship by one stroke.

He was just off the 11th green and preparing to hit a wedge out of deep rough when he said his club touched the ball, causing it to move slightly. Nobody else saw the infringement and the rules officials left it up to him. Bobby was adamant the ball had moved and penalized himself one stroke, despite playing partner Walter Hagen trying to talk him out of it.

He finished the championship in a tie with the Scot Willie Macfarlane. The 18-hole playoff also ended in a tie, and so a further 18 holes were needed to separate them. They came to the 18th all square, but a bogey cost Bobby the title.

Afterwards he was congratulated on his honesty, and Bobby replied, "You might as well congratulate me for not robbing a bank."

At the US Open the following year something similar happened. On the 15th green in the second round, he had placed his putter head behind the ball when a strong wind moved it a fraction. Again, despite nobody having seen it, he called a one-shot penalty on himself.

But this time he ended up winning the championship by a stroke.

Gene Sarazen

Gene's premonition

According to sportswriter OB Keeler, Gene Sarazen says he had a premonition about his famous albatross at the 15th hole at Augusta in the 1935 Masters. It came at the previous hole when he heard the roar of the crowd after Craig Wood's birdie on the 18th green. His playing partner, and great rival, Walter Hagen said to him, "Well, Gene, that looks as if it's all over." "Oh, I don't know," Gene replied. "They might go in from anywhere."

At the next hole, Gene's approach shot hit the far bank of the water hazard and rolled across the putting surface and fell neatly into the hole. When news of the "double eagle" was carried to the clubhouse by an eager runner, not everyone believed him. "Mr. Gene done made a two on 15," the runner said. The response was, "No, you've got the holes wrong, 16 is a par-3." But the runner said, "No, Mr. Gene done made a two on 15."

One of the witnesses to the great shot was Bobby Jones, who had wandered down to the 15th green because, like many at the time, he was fascinated by the Sarazen–Hagen rivalry. Gene tied Wood after 72 holes, but the next day beat him by five shots in a playoff. Meanwhile, the ball and club Gene used that day are in the Trophy Room at Augusta.

Gary Player

You can quote me on that

Gary Player said he was practising in a bunker in Texas one day when a man wearing a big Stetson stood and watched for a few minutes. Gary holed his bunker shot and the man made a $50 bet with him that he couldn't hole the next one. Gary duly did, and so the stranger doubled down on his bet, and offered him $100 that he couldn't hole three in a row. Sure enough, Gary holed out again. As the man peeled off the dollar bills and handed them to Gary, he said, "Boy, I've never seen anyone so lucky in my life." To which Gary replied, "Well, the harder I practise, the luckier I get."

This quote remains one of the most famous in golf, and it has stayed with Gary his whole life. Certainly, when it came to bunker play, Gary had few equals. However, he admits he didn't invent the quote. In his book *Gary Player's Golf Secrets*, published in 1962, he attributes the quote to fellow golfer Jerry Barber, the previous year's winner of the USPGA Championship.

Barber was noted for his quick wit, and when a friend called him lucky, he shot back with, "Yes, and the harder I practise, the luckier I get." Incidentally, another well-known golfing aphorism is attributed to Barber: "The older you get, the easier it is to shoot your age."

Tom Lehman

Born 1959

Always the bridesmaid...

For four successive years, Tom Lehman played in the last group in the US Open. And every time he watched someone else be crowned champion. His Groundhog Day of heartbreak began in 1995 at Shinnecock Hills. One shot off eventual champion Corey Pavin's lead, Tom found the fairway bunker at the 16th. He eventually made the green in four and two-putted for a bogey. "I hit a bad drive and it cost me the tournament," Tom said.

In 1996, he was tied for the lead with Steve Jones playing the last at Oakland Hills. He thought he had hit a perfect drive, only for the ball to take a wicked bounce and finish in a bunker. "When I hit it, I was pretty happy with it," Tom said. "I hit it just the way I wanted to." After laying up, he made bogey, and Jones won the title by a single shot. However, Tom compensated for that disappointment by winning the Open at Royal Lytham the following month.

At Congressional in 1997, he was tied for the lead until he made a bogey on the 16th. He was forced to take on the flag at the 17th but hit his approach with a 7-iron heavy and the ball found water. "That's the shot I wish I had over," Tom admitted.

He can be excused defeat at Olympic Club in 1998. He started the final round three behind Lee Janzen and finished six adrift.

Retief Goosen

Born 1969

Bolt from the blue

Retief Goosen, the 2001 and 2004 US Open champion, knows how close he came to not having a golf career at all. In 1985, when he was just 15, he was playing with his cousin Henri at Pietersburg Golf Club, in his native South Africa, when a sudden bolt of lightning struck a tree and bounced onto him. Henri said later, "His tongue was down his throat and his eyes were backward, and he was breathing weird. He had no clothes on; they'd been burned from his body. I was screaming for help."

As luck would have it, a doctor was playing the next hole and ran to Retief's aid. "He brought me back to life," Retief said. His shoes had disintegrated from his feet, and his underwear and watch band had melted into his body. Retief says he remembers nothing until he woke up in hospital, covered in bandages, where he spent the next six days. Then he was back out onto the golf course. His father Theo took it as a sign that Retief was destined for great things as a golfer.

The incident has left Retief with partial hearing loss in his left ear and an irregular heartbeat. Meanwhile, the clothes he was wearing that day – a blue polo shirt, ripped to shreds, and a pair of brown chinos with its left leg torn off – are on display in the World Golf Hall of Fame.

Tom Watson

An invitation from the King

Tom Watson says the most important golf tournament he ever won was the 1964 Kansas City Men's Matchplay when he was 14 because it brought him to the attention of two of the greatest players in the game, giving him the impetus to pursue a career as a professional. A year after his matchplay success, he was sitting with his mother in their den at home when the phone rang. His mother answered it. "Just a minute, I'll have to ask him," she said down the line. She then turned to her son and said, "Tommy, would you like to play with Arnold Palmer?"

"Are you kidding?" was Tom's reply. Arnie was his hero and the two of them played an exhibition match. They both shot two under for the front nine. Tom had an old brass-headed PG150 putter back then, and after a birdie on the 1st, sank a long, snaking putt on the 4th. "Let me have a look at that," Arnie said, taking the putter. "That's pretty good," he said.

The following year, aged 16, Tom came home from school and received another phone call. This time it was an invitation to play with Jack Nicklaus. During the pre-match clinic, he watched in disbelief at how high Nicklaus was able to hit his long irons, prompting Tom to go back to his coach Stan Thirsk and reconstruct his swing – a swing he used to win eight major championships.

"To play well you must feel tranquil and at peace. I have never been troubled by nerves in golf because I felt I had nothing to lose and everything to gain."

Harry Vardon

Mickey Wright

1935–2020

The Wright stuff

By the time injury forced Mickey Wright to retire in 1969, aged just 34, she had won 82 events on the LPGA Tour and 13 major championships. Ben Hogan said she had the most beautiful golf swing, man or woman, in the history of the game.

On 16 June 2012, the USGA opened the Mickey Wright Room at their headquarters in New Jersey. It's an archive of the life and career of arguably the greatest ever female player. It contains her Wilson clubs, the Bullseye putter she used to win all but one of her majors, her practice mat, her extensive music collection, and the typewriter on which she wrote her national newspaper column.

Mickey was always a very private person. When she retired, she retreated to her South Florida home, and seldom gave interviews. After her death in 2020, her ashes were placed in the bay window in the room that bears her name. She bequeathed her entire estate to the USGA and when the museum curators went to her home they discovered a treasure trove of memorabilia, including notebooks full of swing thoughts; video tapes of her greatest victories; photographs; audiocassettes of conversations with historians and with other great golfers; her LPGA membership cards dating back to 1955; and even plane ticket stubs. Her red shag bag, white golf shoes and a rusty spectator seat were found in the laundry room.

Harry Vardon

1870–1937

Blown off course

In 1920, a 50-year-old Harry Vardon was three shots clear of the field with seven holes to play in the US Open at Inverness Country Club, in Toledo. He had his first major championship for six years in his sights, and a second US Open title, 20 years after his first.

This is when a storm swept across the course. It took Harry four full woods to reach the par-5 12th hole, he missed a two-foot par putt at the 13th, three-putted the 14th, 15th and 16th holes, and then drew a cruel stroke of luck at the 17th when his ball failed to clear a ditch at the front of the green by a matter of inches. He made a double bogey. He now needed a birdie at the last hole to tie Ted Ray, but had to settle for a par.

In the first two rounds of the championship Harry played with an 18-year-old Bobby Jones, who was overawed to be playing with such a legend. On the 7th hole, they both had short chips to the green. Harry hit his close, but Jones skulled his over the back and into a bunker. He made five, and in an attempt to relieve his embarrassment, said to Harry as they walked off the green, "Did you ever see a worse shot than that?"

Harry, who had a reputation for being a little brusque, simply said, "No," and strode to the next tee.

Andy North

Born 1950

Battling adversity

Andy North took up golf by accident. As a schoolboy he was into a variety of sports – basketball, football, baseball – but golf wasn't one of them. It all changed in seventh grade when he was diagnosed with a bone disease, osteochondritis dissecans. A part of his left knee was degenerating because there wasn't adequate blood supply. He spent two years on crutches and his favourite sports were off limits. But his doctor allowed him to play golf, as long as he used a cart and kept his weight off his left leg. He took to it well. Two years later he won the Wisconsin state high school golf championship.

He went on to win three times in 23 years on the PGA Tour – two of which happened to be US Opens, in 1978 and 1985. He doesn't think he got the credit he deserved for his Open wins, but who knows how many more events, how many more majors, he might have bagged but for a chronic injury record. He'd had 12 operations – six on his knees, one on his elbow, one on his neck and four for skin cancer – by the time he played his last US Open in 1995 at Shinnecock Hills, where he had to walk backwards up the steep hills at the 9th, 14th and 15th holes to ease the pain in his knees.

Fuzzy Zoeller

Local knowledge

When Fuzzy Zoeller won the Masters on his debut appearance in 1979, he was assigned the local caddie Jariah "Jerry" Beard, who had been at Augusta National for 22 years and knew every grain and contour like the back of his hand. "He led me round like a seeing-eye dog," Fuzzy said later.

Beard was so knowledgeable on the greens he could read putts from the middle of the fairways. Fuzzy was involved in a sudden death playoff with Tom Watson and Ed Snead, and on the second extra hole, the 11th, Fuzzy hit an 8-iron from 150 yards to eight feet. "That's a right-edge putt," Beard informed his man. "Concentrate on your speed." Fuzzy said Beard did that all week.

Earlier, at the 15th in regulation play, Fuzzy hit the shot of the tournament. He was in the fairway, 235 yards from the green. The rule of thumb back then was if you can see the water in front of the green, go for it with your second shot. If you can't, lay up. Fuzzy said he couldn't see it. "Get on my shoulders and tell me if you can see it now," Beard joked. "We gotta go." Zoeller jumped up onto his tippy toes and could just make out the water. "All right, let's go," he said. He hit his 3-wood onto the green and two-putted for a priceless birdie.

Matt Fitzpatrick

Born 1994

Bunker brilliance

It's been described as the greatest bunker shot in the history of the US Open, and yet Matt Fitzpatrick, who played the stroke at the 18th hole at Brookline, in Boston, helping him to win the championship in 2022, said that bunker play had not been the strongest part of his game.

At least, it hadn't been until he received a tip a few weeks earlier from Paul Azinger, who advised Matt to play long bunker shots with the ball set to the toe of the club, meaning at impact the heel digs into the sand while the toe slides.

Coincidentally, Zinger was on commentary for NBC when Matt hooked his drive into the bunker at the 18th. He called it "a huge mistake". But then, perhaps remembering the tip he had given Matt, added, "It wouldn't surprise me if he pulled this off."

Matt's ball was behind a grassy knoll, which he took out of play by aiming well left and fading it back. Choking down on the grip, he hit "one of the best shots I ever hit". The ball finished about 30 feet above the pin, although he confessed later that it contained an element of "hit and hope". In the commentary box, Zinger said, "What a pressure shot!" About 20 minutes later, Matt's playing partner Will Zalatoris missed a putt to force a playoff, and Matt was US Open champion.

Jack Burke

1923–2024

Divine intervention?

On the Sunday of the 1956 Masters, Jack Burke went to church. Whatever the nature of his communion with God that morning, given that he was eight shots behind leader Ken Venturi he probably thought it futile asking for divine help, the size of the deficit beyond even the powers of the Almighty.

A few hours later, having clawed his way through the field, Jackie stood over a downhill 30-foot putt for birdie on the 17th green to tie the lead. "It was lightning quick," he said. "I never hit a putt more softly in my life. I immediately thought, 'Oh no, I didn't get it halfway to the hole'."

The weather at Augusta that year was cold and windy, and the greens were dried to concrete. Dow Finsterwald said they had been cut so short you could hear the ball roll. On another day, Jackie's putt on the 17th might have finished halfway to the hole, from where another two putts would have been the likely outcome. But nature had other plans. "A gust of wind came up and took the ball with it," Jackie remembered. "That ball kept rolling and rolling and rolling until it dropped in the centre of the cup. It was a miracle."

With Venturi imploding behind him, Jackie holed a tricky four-foot putt on the 18th for a round of 71, containing only 29 putts, and victory by one shot.

Lee Trevino

Driving violation

In the 1974 Open at Royal Lytham, Lee Trevino was paired with the Australian Bruce Devlin in the last round. They had both been playing very poorly and were well down the field. On the driving range before their starting time, Lee noticed that Devlin was spraying his drives left and right. "Hell, I'm gonna be spending all day looking for your golf balls," Lee said.

At the time, Lee was using a MacGregor driver with a nickel insert and he gave it to Devlin to try. At once, Devlin's driving accuracy improved. "That's great," Lee said, to which Devlin replied, "Yeah, but what's it going to do for me?" So, they came up with a plan.

At Open Championships, every group has an official with them, and when Lee had the honour, he would hit his drive, and then while the official was busy looking to see where the ball had gone, he would surreptitiously hand his driver to Devlin, and Devlin would hand him his. They continued this way for the entire round.

Afterwards, at an R&A dinner, Lee told an official that this is what they had done. He could see the official wasn't impressed. "What are you going to do?" Lee said. "Not pay me? I couldn't buy a steak with what I won that day."

"When you see that many people with a smile on their face, then you must be doing something right."

Greg Norman

Walter Hagen

Clocking on

At a time when people looked down their noses at professional golfers, many golf clubs wouldn't allow them into their clubhouses unless they used the back door – and once inside, the facilities were strictly out of bounds.

This rule infuriated Walter Hagen. When Royal Cinque Ports, in Deal, denied him entry to the clubhouse before the 1920 Open he hired a Daimler, complete with chauffeur, and parked it on the front drive of the club. He changed his shoes and clothes in the car and ate his meals on the back seat: pheasant, caviar and smoked salmon, washed down with champagne.

A month later, attitudes towards professionals changed. The setting for the 1920 US Open was Inverness Country Club, in Toledo. Breaking with tradition, the members welcomed amateurs and professionals alike into the clubhouse, allowing all the competitors to eat their meals together in the dining room. The club also found rooms for the pros and arranged cars to and from the course.

After the championship, Walter and a group of professionals, which included the newly crowned champion Ted Ray, clubbed together to buy Inverness a seven-foot grandfather clock as a mark of their appreciation of a gesture that helped break down the class barriers in golf. Today it stands proudly in the clubhouse foyer and bears the inscription: "God measures men by what they are/Not by what they in wealth possess/This vibrant message chimes afar/The voice of Inverness."

Lee Janzen

Born 1964

Lucky breaks

Look at Lee Janzen's scorecard on the final day of the 1998 US Open at the Olympic Club, San Francisco, and it says he made a regulation par at the 5th hole on his way to his second national Open title. But that tells only a part of the story.

He was five behind Payne Stewart when he pushed his drive at the 457-yard par-4, which doglegs right amid a thick row of trees. As they searched for the ball a marshal said he had followed the ball flight with his binoculars, and it had stayed in a tree. So, Lee made his way disconsolately back to the tee only for the ball to drop out of the tree. He chipped onto the fairway, and despite hitting his third over the green, holed an unlikely chip for par. He said later, "I was thinking I might make six or seven and I made four. Anyone would walk away from that feeling great about themselves."

Luck smiled on him again at the 11th where he tugged an 8-iron into the rough to the left of the green. But the ball kicked off the hill and settled just 12 feet from the hole, from where he sank the putt to narrow the deficit to two. A short while later, Lee took the lead after a par at the 16th and held on to win by a shot.

Louis Oosthuizen

Born 1982

The Bland Slam

It's not an achievement golfers aspire to, but nine golfers in the history of the game have finished runner-up in all four major championships: Jack Nicklaus, Arnold Palmer, Tom Watson, Phil Mickelson, Greg Norman, Dustin Johnson, Jason Day, Craig Wood and Louis Oosthuizen.

Oosthuizen's Grand Slam of Seconds (or the Bland Slam, as one broadcaster called it) started in 2012 when he was beaten in a playoff for the Masters by Bubba Watson. Runners-up berths followed in successive majors in 2015, the US Open and the Open (the latter in another playoff, to Zach Johnson). He completed the unwanted set at the 2017 PGA Championship.

Following his tied second place at Quail Hollow in 2017, on the flight home the usually phlegmatic South African embarked on some seriously committed lip-syncing to the Andra Day song "Rise Up", later posting the clip to his Twitter/X account. Understandably, it went viral. "I'll rise up/Rise like the day/I'll rise up/I'll rise up unafraid", Louis mimed, inferring that he was not going to be too downbeat after this latest near miss, and that he was convinced better times lay ahead.

However, two more runners-up positions lay in wait for Louis four years later when he finished second to Jon Rahm at the US Open and to Phil Mickelson at the PGA Championship.

Hale Irwin

Born 1945

Irwin's air shot

Ask Hale Irwin which shot he would like to have again, and he wouldn't hesitate. The air shot, or "whiff", may have cost him the 1983 Open at Royal Birkdale.

At the 14th hole in the third round, Hale was gaining ground on the leaders. He left his birdie try at the par-3 two inches short, and then, inexplicably, as he nonchalantly tried to tap the ball into the hole, made an air shot. He quickly backhanded the ball into the cup and then turned to his playing partner, Terry Gale, and said, "I made four." He tried to explain it afterwards. "I looked up. And in one motion the putter hit the ground, moved forward and over the ball."

Hale was so shaken he bogeyed the next hole, the par-5 15th, one of the easiest on the course. He finished with a one-over 72, four behind Tom Watson. He seemed to put the disappointment behind him because on Sunday he shot one of the rounds of the day, a 67, and then waited to see if he had done enough to win the Claret Jug.

It all came down to Watson, who had two putts on the 18th to win by one from Hale and Andy Bean. Hale prayed Watson would make a birdie to render his gaffe the previous day irrelevant. But Watson two-putted for par and victory, leaving Hale to ponder what might have been.

Dustin Johnson

Rules controversy No. 2

Dustin Johnson won the 2016 US Open at Oakmont, Pennsylvania, by three shots, but his last round of 69 was mired in a rules controversy. At the 5th hole, DJ faced an uphill four-foot par putt. As was his routine, he put the toe of the putter near the ball and about two seconds later it moved fractionally backwards. He called in referee Mark Newell and told him what happened. DJ was adamant, as was his playing partner Lee Westwood, that he had not caused the ball to move. Newell told him to play on with no penalty.

But after a video review, it was decided that the first ruling was made hastily and that DJ might have caused the ball to move after all. Thomas Pagel, the USGA's senior director of Rules of Golf and Amateur Status, said, "We had evidence. We saw it. We had to act on it." By the time he and a USGA colleague caught up with DJ he was on the 12th tee. Westwood said, "I listened in. They didn't ask for any input from me. I thought that was strange." They told DJ a decision would be made at the end of his round, meaning he played the last seven holes of the championship not knowing where he stood in relation to the rest of the field, and vice versa.

In the end, he was penalized a stroke, but still won by three.

Juli Inkster

Born 1960

Inkster is irked

It's the ones that get away that continue to rankle with golfers long after the final putts have dropped. Juli Inkster won seven majors in her career, but the US Women's Open at Oakmont in 1992 still gives her sleepless nights.

It featured a great last day duel between Juli and her close friend Patty Sheehan. Playing the 17th, Juli held a two-stroke lead. However, shortly after playing their tee shots, a storm swept through the course, forcing a weather delay. When play resumed, Sheehan birdied the 17th to trim Juli's lead to one.

At the 18th, Juli's drive was in the fairway, while Sheehan's ball found the rough. Sheehan then called over a rules official and to Juli's fury was allowed to take a drop in the fairway, the nearest point of relief. Sheehan said she could see Juli was "incensed". Juli said later, "She'd been granted relief from casual water, which didn't strike me as possible because she was on a sideslope and any water would have flowed away."

Sheehan hit her approach to 15 feet and made the birdie putt, while Juli could only make par. Sheehan won the next day's 18-hole playoff by two strokes. Juli said, "I don't mind saying that rules officials in that period were weak. Years later, that official told me that if she had it to do over, she wouldn't have granted relief. I still think about it. It burns me up."

"When you're the best, and you know you're the best, and your contemporaries know you're the best, that's a terrific edge."

Ray Floyd

Jack Nicklaus

Mother's Day

In 1986, Jack Nicklaus' mother Helen said she wanted to go to Augusta National to see her son play in the Masters "one more time before I pass". Every year, Jack's father Charlie went with his friends and Helen considered it a trip for the boys. Her one and only previous visit was in 1959, when she went with Jack's sister Marilyn and his future wife Barbara. Jack was still an amateur and in his first Masters missed the cut.

Helen couldn't have picked a better year than 1986. Marilyn went too, also her first time since 1959, and remembers her 78-year-old mother almost running up the hill to the 17th green on the last day. Jack had knocked the ball to 15 feet, and Helen wanted to see if Jack could sink the birdie putt to lead the Masters. He made it, of course, and his post-putt celebration, left foot forward and putter raised heavenwards, is one of the most iconic images in Masters history.

Jack won his sixth green jacket at the age of 46 despite Helen thinking her presence might jinx him. Understandably she was elated. Marilyn said, "He had given her a gift she would never forget."

The next day, Helen drove home to Ohio with Marilyn and her family. Marilyn said they were all singing in the car. "That week was special," she said. "I think Mom being there was in Jack's mind. It was meant to be."

Bobby Jones

Old Course love affair

Bobby Jones had a love–hate relationship with the Old Course at St Andrews. His first visit was as a 19-year-old for the Open in 1921 and the championship began promisingly. Rounds of 78 and 74 put him five behind leader Jock Hutchison. But in the third round he took 46 to the turn and then at the 11th hole took four shots to escape the notorious Hill bunker and disqualified himself.

He put it down to the petulance of youth. "I was unable to understand the reverence with which the place was regarded by our British friends," he said later. "I considered St Andrews among the very worst courses I had ever seen."

His impression of St Andrews changed over the years. He won the Open there in 1927 and made a triumphant return three years later, winning the Amateur Championship over the old links, the first major title in his Grand Slam year.

Six years after his retirement, he stopped off at St Andrews on his way to Berlin for the Summer Olympics. He said, "Of all the courses I have played in this country, I think St Andrews is the best, and it is worth the trip across the Atlantic to visit once more." He only played an informal round but 5,000 people were reported to have come out and seen him shoot a level par round of 72, which included just 32 on the front nine.

Gary Player

Muirfield miracle

At the halfway stage of the 1959 Open at Muirfield, Gary Player was eight shots off the lead. Few people gave him a chance of winning, but the night before the final day's 36 holes he told a friend he had a feeling something special would happen. "Tomorrow you're going to see a miracle," he said. "I'm going to win the British Open."

A third round 70 brought him into contention, and then in the afternoon, he played one of the rounds of his life. Standing on the 18th tee six under for the day, and with one hand on the Claret Jug, he hit his drive into a pot bunker and ended up taking a double-bogey six. Gary was convinced he'd blown his chance. He went back to his hotel, remembering how Sam Snead blew the 1939 US Open with a triple bogey on the 72nd hole, and never won his national open.

But the leaders struggled in the windy conditions. Fred Bullock and Flory Van Donck needed birdies at the last to tie Gary but they both made bogey fives and finished two adrift. At 23, Gary became the youngest winner of the Open since Young Tom Morris in 1868.

In those days, the champion was responsible for engraving the trophy. When Gary brought the Claret Jug back the following year, the R&A noticed his name had been engraved a little larger than any of the previous winners.

Hal Sutton

Born 1958

Powerhouse pairing?

As Ryder Cup captain of the American team at Oakland Hills in 2004, Hal Sutton famously paired together Tiger Woods and Phil Mickelson, the two best golfers on the planet at the time, for the first day's matches.

Hal admits his vice-captains tried to dissuade him. "Tiger and Phil weren't the best friends at the time," Hal admitted later. But he made the decision, he said, to teach them a lesson about teamwork. "If they leave better friends, golf is the winner," he added. Tiger and Phil lost both their matches. Hal didn't pair them up again, and the American team were eventually thrashed 18½-9½. It was a chastening experience for Hal. "I pretty much quit golf after that. I took the blame for everything," he said.

Phil brought the subject up on the eve of the 2016 Ryder Cup. He said Hal only gave him and Tiger two days' notice that they were playing together, and given they played with different types of ball, Phil didn't have enough time to learn how to play with the high-spin ball Tiger favoured. He said Hal "put us in a position to fail and we failed monumentally".

Hal hit back. He claimed Phil changed his equipment, including his ball, just prior to the 2004 matches. "He let his whole team down," he said. "They didn't beat anybody. So, it couldn't be their fault. It had to be Hal Sutton's fault."

Ben Hogan

Ben's Triple Crown

Ben Hogan's victory at Carnoustie was his third major triumph of the year, after wins at Augusta in April, and then at the US Open at Oakmont in June. His thoughts now would surely turn to the PGA Championship, and the possibility of a Grand Slam.

Unfortunately, this wasn't possible. The PGA Championship had been and gone, and Ben hadn't been able to play in it. Qualifying for the Open – and yes, even someone of the calibre of Ben Hogan, with two majors already tucked away that year, had to qualify – took place at the same time as the PGA at Birmingham Country Club, in Alabama.

It's very possible Ben wouldn't have played the PGA anyway, even if the scheduling had allowed him to. He won it twice, in 1946 and 1948, but since his car accident he had skipped it, believing the toil of playing 36 holes of matchplay for five successive days would be too much for him. He played it three more times in the 1960s but only after the championship switched to strokeplay. So, Ben never got a shot at the ultimate prize in professional golf.

Greg Norman

Making love to his fingers

Greg Norman won the first of his two Open Championships at Turnberry in 1986, and he revealed afterwards that a tip Jack Nicklaus had given him helped him over the line.

After three rounds, Greg led the field by one (he led all four majors after 54 holes that year, prompting one American golf writer to dub it the "Saturday Slam"). In his hotel room on Sunday morning, he picked up a club and started swinging. He realized his left hand was too tight on the grip and was reminded of a conversation he had had with Nicklaus the previous evening, who had advised him to grip the club as lightly as possible. He heeded Nicklaus' advice and struck the ball as well as ever. His final round of 69 won him the Claret Jug by five shots. As soon as Greg walked off the 18th green, Nicklaus, who had been in the TV commentary box, reached down and congratulated the new Open champion.

From then on, whenever Greg got under pressure in a tournament, he would say to himself, "Make love to your fingers" and he would caress his fingertips, and it relieved the pressure in his neck and all the way down to his forearms.

Phil Mickelson

Foodie Phil

The host of the Champions Dinner at Augusta on the eve of the 2014 Masters was the defending champion Adam Scott and his menu had an Antipodean theme. For dessert he served pavlova and as it came out of the kitchen Phil Mickelson started talking about the history of the dish. He said it was named after the great ballerina Anna Pavlova after she had toured Australia and New Zealand in the 1920s. A chef was so taken with her beauty and grace he created a meringue-based dish, with fresh fruit and cream, in her honour.

People around the table shook their heads. Chairman Billy Payne looked at Phil as if to say, what kind of stuff are you spewing here. Zach Johnson said, "I got $100 that's not right." But because cell phones are banned at the Champions Dinner, nobody was able to find out for sure.

Phil said, "Everybody was calling me out on my BS, and a lot of the time I am BS-ing." However, he was sure of the facts, because as he revealed later his daughter had been a dancer and wrote a dissertation at school on Anna Pavlova. Phil said he even made 32 pavlovas for every member of her class.

Gene Littler

1930–2019

Comeback kid

In March 1972, a routine doctor's appointment turned out to be anything but routine for Gene Littler. An ominous lump was found in his left armpit, diagnosed as a malignant tumour of the lymph gland. He had an operation to remove muscle mass on the left side of his body. He made his peace with knowing he might never play again, but then he'd had a great career, winning the US Amateur in 1953, the US Open eight years later, and playing on six Ryder Cup teams.

His recovery was slow and painful. At first he couldn't lift a one-pound barbell off his kitchen table. The first time he tried hitting golf balls, he shanked every one of them. But 15 months after the operation, Gene "The Machine" won a tour event again. It was the most gratifying and emotional win of his career. "I realized I was the only player who had ever come back from that kind of surgery," he said.

He should have won the USPGA Championship in 1977. Aged 47, he stood on the 10th tee on the back nine on Sunday at Pebble Beach, California, with a five-shot lead, only to make five bogeys in six holes and finish in a tie with Lanny Wadkins. In the first sudden death playoff in major championship golf, Wadkins won on the third extra hole. "Sudden death stinks," Gene said later.

"I push myself to be the best I can be. I don't worry about what other people are doing, and I don't think about things I can't control."

Annika Sörenstam

Payne Stewart

My wife, my putting coach

Payne Stewart won the US Open at Pinehurst in 1999 thanks to a remarkable putting display over the last three holes on Sunday. He made a 30-foot par putt on the 16th, a four-foot birdie putt on the 17th, and then, crucially, an 18-footer for par, and victory, on the last green.

Afterwards he thanked the person who had given him a valuable putting tip on the eve of the last round – his wife, Tracey. "Keep your head still," she had told him, which is as basic a putting tip as you can get, but Payne understood its importance. He wasn't happy with his touch on the greens on Saturday, and Tracey said she had been watching him and noticed that he had been moving his head. So, he worked on the problem on the putting green that evening.

Tracey admitted that the tip initially came from Payne's late father, who had sent her a letter shortly before his death in 1985 with a list of things to look out for in his son's game. One of them was lifting his head while putting. She framed the letter and would refer to it when Payne was in the heat of competition.

Annika Sörenstam

Comeback Queen

Annika Sörenstam set a lot of records in her career. In 2001, just a month after a record-breaking 59 and having bagged her third major at the Nabisco Championship, she recorded the largest comeback victory on the LPGA Tour at the Office Depot tournament at Wilshire Country Club, Los Angeles, beating the previous record held by Muffin Spencer-Devlin in 1985.

In this 54-hole event, Annika began the final round ten shots behind the overnight leader Pat Hurst. The only player within six shots of the lead was Liselotte Neumann. Annika made seven birdies and one bogey for a round of 66, compared to Hurst's 77, to tie the lead with Mi Hyun Kim, who shot a 65. Annika then beat the South Korean player at the first extra hole.

At the same time, Annika's first-place prize money of $120,000 took her past Betsy King as the tour's all-time leading money winner, a position she still holds.

After the event, Annika said, "I needed a miracle, and I got it. I just can't believe it's happening to me this year. I don't know if I really deserve all this." She won a total of eight events on the LPGA Tour in 2001 and predictably finished top of the money list.

Four years later, Annika tied the record for consecutive victories in scheduled events – four – set by Nancy Lopez in 1978, and then equalled by Nelly Korda in 2024.

Scottie Scheffler

Born 1996

Mallet makes a difference

From tee to green at the 2024 Genesis Invitational at
Riviera Country Club, in Los Angeles, Scottie Scheffler
was killing it. On the greens, however, he was last in the
field. Rory McIlory, who was a guest analyst for CBS, had
just watched Scottie miss a ten-footer and was asked by
reporter Amanda Renner if he had any advice for him.

"I'd love to see Scottie try a mallet," McIlroy said. He
was speaking from experience. He had struggled with
a blade putter himself in the past, saying he felt his
stroke needed to be "so perfect" to start the ball where
he wanted. But when he switched to a mallet putter,
however, he found the consistency on the greens he was
looking for. He thought the mallet gave him "a little bit
more margin for error".

The following week, at the Bay Hill Invitational,
Scottie put a TaylorMade Spider Tour putter, similar to
the one McIlroy uses, in his bag. He won the tournament
by five shots, ranking fifth on the greens. In the ensuing
months he also won the Players Championship, his
second Masters title, the RBC Heritage, the Memorial
Tournament, the Travellers Championship and an
Olympic gold medal. Scottie claimed he didn't hear
McIlroy's advice, and that he was thinking about making
the switch anyway, but that didn't stop McIlroy saying,
"I'm not going to give him any more advice, that's
for sure."

Arnold Palmer

Arnie rules OK

Arnold Palmer's first major title was the Masters in 1958, and it didn't come without a huge amount of controversy.

He and Ken Venturi came to the par-3 12th in the final round with Arnie leading by one. The wind was swirling, as it so often is in that corner of the course, and they both flew the green into the bank at the back. Venturi's ball rolled down to the fringe, from where he two-putted for par.

Arnie's ball plugged, and he believed he should have been allowed a drop. They were playing wet-weather rules which permitted balls to be lifted, cleaned and replaced.

Arnie was dumbstruck when an official told him he had to play it as it lay. He couldn't advance it more than 18 inches, and then needed three more to get down. Convinced he had received an incorrect ruling, Arnie went back and dropped another ball where the first ball had plugged and made par.

On the 13th tee, he didn't know if he was still a shot ahead of Venturi, or one behind. Nevertheless, at the par-5, a superb 3-wood from the fairway found the putting surface, and a few minutes later he rolled in a 20-foot putt for eagle.

On the 15th, he got word that the three with his provisional ball at the 12th would stand. Despite dropped shots at the 16th and 18th Arnie won the Masters by a single shot.

Johnny Miller

Showing off

In 1986, *Golf Digest* writer Guy Yocom witnessed Johnny Miller's iron play brilliance at the launch of Spalding's new golf ball, the Tour Edition. Spalding had recruited its three best staff players, Greg Norman, Craig Stadler and Miller to hit some shots to a flag 155 yards away to demonstrate the qualities of its new soft-feel ball.

Yocom said Stadler went first and the crowd of about 50 were impressed with his control, and the spin he was able to exert. Several shots stopped within six feet of the flag. Norman went next, and he hit fades, draws and straight shots, each one spinning exactly as he predicted.

Last up was Johnny. He hadn't seen what Norman and Stadler had done because he was chatting to someone in the crowd. Yocom said he hit every type of shot in the book, and a few that weren't – some low, others soaring onto the green from a great height. He hit high loopy shots, he purposely hit a couple thin, others he hit with a great curve, left and right, as though avoiding an invisible tree. They all stopped on a sixpence next to the hole. Two hit the flag, another lipped out. The crowd was stunned into silence.

Afterwards he turned to Norman and Stadler and said, "How would you guys like to do this for money? $50 a shot?" They both sunk back into their chairs and said nothing.

Sam Snead

Battle of the sexes

Sam Snead remains the only man to have won an event on the LPGA Tour. Yes, you read that right. In 1962, Sam won an event on the women's tour, a feat which – not surprisingly – has never been repeated.

A year earlier, Sam received an invitation to play the Royal Poinciana Plaza Invitational at the Palm Beach Par-3 Golf Course, in Florida, which was an official LPGA event. The field was made up of 24 players, men and women, pros and amateurs, and was billed as a Battle of the Sexes. The idea was that by playing the event on a par-3 course it eliminated power and placed the emphasis on precision iron play and putting.

Sam finished third, two strokes behind local pro Walker Allen Pagan Jr and Louise Suggs, one of the founders of the LPGA Tour.

The following year he was invited back, although the format had changed. He was now the only male entrant in a field that included LPGA luminaries such as Mickey Wright, Kathy Whitworth, Patty Berg and Betsy Rawls.

Sam shot a two-day, four-round total of 211, five under par, and finished five shots clear of Wright in second place. After his round, Sam said, "The pressure was double this time. The man is expected to win," although he heaped praise on Wright at the same time, saying she was good enough to compete on the PGA Tour.

José María Olazábal

The pain and the glory

José María Olazábal thought he might have to give up the game when he was at his peak due to chronic pain in his feet. In 1996, he watched the Masters from his sofa. He had won the green jacket two years earlier, but now it hurt to even stand.

The pain was so intense at the start of the 1995 season he took an 18-month sabbatical from golf which meant having to miss the Ryder Cup. The first doctor he saw said he had rheumatoid arthritis and advised rest, treatment and a lot of patience. Ollie swam every day, walked on sand and exercised by stretching his toes.

It didn't help. He saw another doctor who told him a biomechanical problem caused by a lower back hernia was responsible and prescribed injections of iron, zinc, amino acids and shark cartilage.

He made his return to competitive golf in February 1997, finishing 12th in the Dubai Desert Classic. The following month Ollie won the Turespaña Masters, in Gran Canaria. He wept, although this time his tears were of joy and not of pain. "I don't think you have seen me cry many times on the golf course," he said afterwards. "I cried that day."

He didn't have to watch the Masters on TV in 1997. He played in it and finished in a tie for 12th. Two years later, he won his second green jacket.

Ben Crenshaw

Born 1952

Someone watching over you

In 1995, Ben Crenshaw won the Masters with an angel on his shoulder. The Sunday before the tournament started, Ben's coach, mentor and friend Harvey Penick died, aged 90. Ben played a practice round at Augusta on Tuesday, and then the next day he and Tom Kite flew to Austin to be pallbearers at Penick's funeral.

Ben had missed three cuts in four starts, and hadn't broken 70 in two months. But that week Ben said Penick's teachings were with him over every swing and every putt. "It was kind of like I felt this hand on my shoulder, guiding me along," he said. When, in the third round, Ben's ball found the sand at the 8th, it somehow managed to pop out. "Another Harvey bounce," Ben's wife, Julie, said to herself. On Sunday, Ben's drive at the 2nd hit a tree and rebounded into the fairway, from where he made a birdie. "Look, there's Harvey," Julie said to a friend. And then, holding a one-shot lead on the 14th, he hit an 8-iron from under a tree that kicked off a mound and onto the green, 12 feet from the pin.

When Ben holed his winning putt he dropped his putter and bent over and sobbed. He said he had a 15th club in the bag that week. "I don't know how it happened," he said afterwards. But a great many people who were there that day...well, they knew.

"People don't understand that when I grew up, I was never the most talented. I was never the biggest. I was never the fastest. I certainly was never the strongest. The only thing I had was my work ethic, and that's been what has gotten me this far."

Tiger Woods

Tiger Woods

F* the Gators**

At his peak, such was the aura around Tiger Woods that his rivals very often considered themselves a stroke or two in arrears before they had even teed off.

Tiger knew this and wasn't going to dilute his advantage by getting too chummy with them – no joshing in the players' lounge or dining with them in the evening.

It's refreshing then to hear an anecdote that Chris DiMarco recounts that suggests that even in the white heat of battle Woods could display a lighter side.

Woods had a three-stroke lead over DiMarco going into the last round of the 2005 Masters and at one point the pair had the practice range to themselves.

They were practising about 50 yards apart. DiMarco is an alumnus of the University of Florida and an avid fan of the Gators, the college basketball team that had just won the national championships. So, he wrote "Go Gators" on a golf ball and played an immaculate chip shot straight into Woods' bucket of balls.

Woods picked it out and wrote something on the ball, before chipping it back. When DiMarco picked it up he saw that Woods had scratched out "Go" and written in its place "F*** the Gators".

DiMarco still has the ball today.

What he doesn't have, however, is a green jacket. Woods beat him in a playoff later that day for his fourth title, while it was as close as DiMarco ever came.

Justin Rose

Born 1980

Amateur dramatics

"It is the one shot I have tried to live up to and get past."
In 1998, in the final round of the Open at Royal Birkdale,
a 17-year-old amateur called Justin Rose was in a spot of
bother short of the 18th green. He had shot a remarkable
66 in the second round and was destined to finish as
leading amateur, but in his own words he had started
to "butcher" his 72nd hole, his approach going no more
than 40 yards.

"I had to go over one of those pot bunkers, so it was
basically a high lob shot," Justin remembers. When it
went in, he looked up to the heavens, thinking, "oh my
goodness, what have I just done". He finished the
Open tied fourth, the highest finish by an amateur
for 45 years, and was only two shots out of a playoff
for the championship.

When he turned pro the next day it was amid much
media excitement. But he missed his first 21 cuts as a
professional, and Justin admits that "that shot became a
little bit of a burden to me". A Lego fanatic, Jared Jacobs,
even created a Lego scene of Justin's chip. "That's when
you know it was a cool achievement," Justin says.

Justin has lived up to that shot now. He won the US
Open in 2013 and three years later an Olympic gold
medal. And in 2024, aged 43, he almost won the Open
Championship at Royal Troon.

Steve Jones

Born 1958

Grip it and win it

In November 1991, after damaging tendons and ligaments in the ring finger on his left hand in a dirt bike accident, Steve Jones couldn't hit a golf ball for nearly three years. And then, just as it was finally beginning to heal, he damaged his index finger pulling up carpet in his house and was told by doctors he would be out for a further two months. He couldn't bend the finger and rather than wait for it to repair, Steve went back out on tour with a new grip, laying the injured index finger over the top of his right hand. He jokingly called it the reverse-overlap Vardon Jones grip, similar to a standard putting grip.

Results at the end of 1995 and into the following year gave Steve enough confidence for him to state boldly that he was going to win the US Open. But first he had to overcome the Sunday blues. He was playing well the first three days of tournaments, but a bad last round always cost him. His life changed when he read a book by Ben Hogan. He realized that in comparison to the great man he wasn't practising hard enough.

Steve had to qualify for the US Open in 1996, surviving a playoff to get into that, and ended up winning the championship at Oakland Hills, Michigan, to become the first winner for 20 years who had come through sectional qualifying.

Severiano Ballesteros

His biggest regret

In his autobiography, Seve Ballesteros admitted that when he looked back at the Masters in 1986 he couldn't prevent himself "from crying silent tears". In the centre of the 15th fairway in the last round, he held a one-shot lead over Jack Nicklaus. Seve confessed that two holes earlier he had let his thoughts run away with themselves. A fantastic approach at the par-5 13th to eight feet prompted him to turn to his brother Vicente, who was caddying for him
for the week, and shake his hand. When he holed the putt for an eagle he admitted he thought he was going to be the champion.

But on the 15th fairway, he had an awkward lie. His playing partner Tom Kite noticed it was on the downhill side of a small mound. Seve opted to hit a soft 4-iron but caught it fat and the ball found the water in front of the green. A few minutes later he made a bogey six and he finished the tournament two behind the champion Nicklaus.

People have suggested this is where Seve's career lost momentum, and he didn't disagree. "I lose the finishing punch," he told writer Jaime Diaz in 2010. He said the reason his confidence diminished afterwards is because he wanted to win so much for the memory of his father, Baldomero, who had died of lung cancer just a month before the Masters.

Trevor Immelman

Born 1979

Secrets from the Champions Dinner

According to Trevor Immelman, the best Champions Dinner at Augusta National was hosted by Hideki Matsuyama, winner in 2021. He'll never forget the wagyu beef and sushi, he said. "It was unbelievable, just unbelievable." He has a special mention for Adam Scott's surf and turf menu in 2014, not least because it was accompanied by some Penfolds Grange wine which, Trevor said, "would have set him back a little bit".

Unofficially, it's free seating at the Champions Dinner – but Trevor, champion in 2008, says that is never the case. He always sits at the bottom corner of the table, between Scott and Nick Faldo, and directly opposite Vijay Singh. He says Fuzzy Zoeller and Ian Woosnam tell the best stories and if you sit next to them "you'll be laughing the whole night long". He's never sat next to either Jack Nicklaus or Tiger Woods. They sit halfway down the long, rectangular table. Thirty-three majors in adjoining seats.

Trevor says the most uncomfortable person at the dinner is always the champion from two years earlier. As defending champion, and host of the dinner, he sits between the Masters chairman and Ben Crenshaw at the head of the table, but the following year, if he hasn't won before, he doesn't know where to sit and walks up and down the table, looking for a spare seat. "It's really funny to see," Trevor says.

Tom Watson

Pebble's greatest chip

It was one of the most famous chip shots in the history of major championship golf. At the 1982 US Open at Pebble Beach, Tom Watson was once again going head-to-head with his great rival Jack Nicklaus. Tom and Jack were tied for the lead when Tom pulled a 2-iron into the rough to the left of the green at the par-3 17th. "That's dead," he said to his caddie Bruce Edwards, who offered his man a few words of encouragement. "C'mon, let's get it up and down," he said.

When they got to the green, Tom's mood changed. He took the sand wedge from his bag and Edwards said, "Get it close." "Get it close?" Tom replied. "Hell, I'm gonna hole it." He took dead aim and, sure enough, the ball fell into the hole. As Tom ran around the green in celebration, he pointed back at Edwards. "See! Told you so," he said. Nicklaus was watching all this unfold on a monitor, helpless.

It gave Tom a one-shot lead and then, at the 18th, he holed a birdie putt from about 30 feet, giving him his one and only US Open title. As he left the green, Nicklaus, who had seen a fifth national title snatched away, congratulated him. Referring to the Open at Turnberry five years earlier, he said, "You little son-of-a-bitch, you did it to me again."

"Before you take your address, while you're still reading the putt, imagine the ball tracking on the line you've chosen and falling into the cup. If you don't believe you can make every putt, why bother trying?"

Ernie Els

JoAnne Carner

Born 1939

Beat your age

In the first round of the 2023 US Women's Senior Open at Waverley Country Club, in Portland, JoAnne Carner shot 80. For most of the players in the field, this would constitute something of a disaster. But for JoAnne it was a triumph, something to celebrate. She was 84 years old, and it marked the sixth time in this championship that she had either equalled or bettered her age.

She went out in 41, five over par, and after dropping shots on her 10th, 11th and 12th holes, she played the last six in level par, including a tee shot on her closing hole, the 9th, which finished just two feet from the pin. Not that she could see it. "My eyes aren't that good," she said. "But I appreciated the applause. I knew I could finally make a birdie."

JoAnne, or Big Mama as she is known, won two US Women's Opens in her career, in 1971 and 1976. Her competitive spirit never waned in the intervening years. In 2018, she struck the very first tee shot in the inaugural US Women's Senior Open, going on to shoot her age, 79. Having broken the record for the oldest person to play in a USGA tournament in 2021, she then shot her age, 83, in the first and second rounds of the 2022 Senior Open.

She's not ruling out extending this remarkable record, by going even lower.

Jordan Spieth

Guesswork

On the 13th hole of his final round in the 2017 Open at Royal Birkdale, Jordan Spieth was so out of position his caddie had to guess the yardage.

Jordan was tied for the lead with playing partner Matt Kuchar when he sprayed his drive a long way right into the rough. He declared the ball unplayable and then started walking backwards looking for a suitable piece of land to drop the ball. He ended up on the practice range. His caddie Michael Greller kept detailed notes of how Jordan played every hole, and for the 13th he wrote: "Driver, 3-iron from practice range," with an asterisk against it. Then, at the bottom, against the asterisk he wrote, "Practice range shot. No yardage. We guessed 240 yards."

It took a total of 20 minutes from finding the ball to Jordan hitting it. His 3-iron found the front of the green, from where he two-putted for a bogey. Kuchar briefly held the lead, but three birdies and an eagle in the next five holes saw Jordan claim his first Open title by three shots.

Jim Furyk

Putter serendipity

Jim Furyk headed to the 2003 US Open at Olympia Fields, Chicago, high on confidence on the greens. He had had two top-ten finishes in the last three weeks and his backweighted Superline putter was working well.

Then, at the beginning of the week, Dogleg Right Golf, which manufactured the Superline, was told by the USGA that the putter was non-conforming, stating that "the club had a backweight that does not wrap completely around the club". They recommended changes to make the club legal.

Jim was understandably very concerned and in practice on the Monday used a Bettinardi Baby Ben putter. Meanwhile, an emergency appeal tabled by Dogleg Right Golf was rejected and so the company president, Dave Billings, took the Superline to the Nike tour van to have the necessary alterations made.

However, by then Jim had made the decision to continue using the Baby Ben. In the first round, he took just 25 putts and from then on saw little reason to change. He won the title by three shots.

"I liked it for alignment purposes," Jim said afterwards. "I was real comfortable with it and I putted very well with it this week. I made some key putts and some great putts. It's kind of an interesting story."

Henrik Stenson

Born 1976

Driving without a driver

Henrik Stenson has become so proficient with his 3-and 4-wood that he very rarely needs to hit a driver from the tee.

When he won the Tour Championship at East Lake in 2015, he was asked by a member of the press if he even bothered putting a driver in his bag. "No, it's a nice club to lean on when you're standing there calculating your yardages," Henrik joked. "It's nice for that."

His love–hate relationship with a driver goes back to his childhood. He was playing with his father one day and managed to break his driver. He said his father got very upset with him. "I'm not going to buy you a new driver because you've ruined this one," Henrik's dad told the future Open champion.

Henrik says he went to an ATM machine and withdrew all his savings – about $200. "It wiped out all of my pocket money for a good while," he said. He bought himself a new driver and a few months later played a round with some friends. After hitting a bad drive, he said he "casually dropped the driver on the tee" and it snapped. "You know how graphite drivers are, with the vibrations," he said. "If it hits the spot, it doesn't need any force. I didn't tell my dad."

Henrik said he didn't have enough money to replace the shaft, so he got used to playing without a driver.

Craig Stadler

Father and son

In 2003, a 50-year-old Craig Stadler was invited to play the BC Open at Endicott, New York, but didn't have a caddie. He asked his son Chris to carry his bag, who agreed on the condition that his dad would pay him for the week.

Chris was not a golfer and had little interest in the game. In Wednesday's pro-am, Craig told him the bag should be shouldered and not carried by the strap. When they were looking for their partner's ball, to Craig's horror he saw that his son had dropped the bag in the middle of the green.

The next day, Craig berated Chris for walking on Mark O'Meara's line. "He's not even on the green," Chris protested. "So?" Craig said. "You're still on his line." O'Meara stood there, shaking his head.

On the final day, Craig powered his way through the field, until he made a bogey on the 17th. In anger, he slammed his putter into the bag. "What's your problem?" Chris enquired, to which Craig said, "It wasn't the most opportune time to make a bogey, dude." Chris' response was, "Well, you made a birdie at 18 yesterday. Make another one today." Craig did as he was told and made a birdie at the 18th to win by one shot.

Afterwards, Chris said, "How much am I getting paid?" Craig said, "Unless it's too much, you're getting a cheque for $58,000."

"Excuse me?" said Chris.

Ken Venturi

1931–2013

Doctor's orders

In February 1962, Ken Venturi was picking a ball out
of the hole during a tournament when he felt a sharp
pain in his chest. Doctors tried a variety of treatments
but couldn't find anything specific. He was forced to
remodel his swing, making it shorter, quicker and
flatter. "The faster I swing, the quicker it will be over,"
he joked.

He missed cut after cut. Lucrative sponsorship deals
were terminated. He had to beg tournament organizers
for invitations. As one friend said, "What Kenny went
through in those years was like a millionaire going
broke." No one wanted him, and in 1964 not even the
Masters, where he had nearly won in 1956 and 1960.

In June 1964, he found something. After third place in
the Thunderbird Classic won him $6,250, he and his wife
Conni cried down the phone. Two weeks later he came
through qualifying for the US Open at Congressional,
in Maryland. He was six off the lead heading into the
final day's 36 holes. In heat and humidity that topped 100
degrees, he neglected to hydrate during his third round,
and shortly after signing for a 66 collapsed and had to be
carried into the clubhouse. A doctor told him playing on
could prove fatal. He ignored the advice, and with the
doctor walking every hole feeding him salt tablets, Ken
shot a final round of 70 to win by four.

Lee Trevino

A lotta bottle

In 1961, Lee Trevino was mustered out of the US Marines after a four-year stint and returned to his old job as a driving range assistant at Hardy's Pitch-n-Putt, in Dallas. He called himself a "range rat", and in the summer, when it was too hot for people to use the facility, he had it to himself. He practised so hard and his short game got so good, nobody would take him on in a match. So, Lee came up with a novel idea. He taped the neck of a 32-ounce Doctor Pepper bottle and used it as his one and only golf club. He would throw the golf ball up in the air and hit it with the bottle, baseball style. "People would bet me that I couldn't hit the green or make a putt," Lee said. "And I usually won the bets."

Once, he shot 29, two over par, with that bottle. He said he could hit it 100 yards, and the longest hole on the course was 120 yards and the shortest 55 yards. On the greens, he put the ball between his legs and putted one-handed, croquet-style. "No yips there, baby," Lee said.

"Golf is the loneliest sport. You're completely alone with every conceivable opportunity to defeat yourself. Golf brings out your assets and liabilities as a person. The longer you play, the more certain you are that a man's performance is the outward manifestation of who, in his heart, he really thinks he is."

Greg Norman

Walter Hagen

Changing of the guard

At the 1920 Open at Royal Cinque Ports, despite finishing 26 shots behind the winner, something in Walter Hagen's game caught the eye of the six-times champion Harry Vardon, who predicted Walter would win several Open titles in his career.

Two years later, when he arrived at Royal St George's, no American-born player had won the Open. Walter had a two-stroke lead at the halfway stage but when a 79 dropped him three back with 18 holes to play it seemed as though the British dominance of their national championship would continue.

But then Walter shot a 72 in the final round and now the only man who could stop him was George Duncan. Starting an hour after the American, the Scot needed an improbable 68 to tie. He played some of the best golf of his life over the back nine and required a par at the last to take the Open into extra holes. But his approach shot at the 18th rolled off the green, followed by a weak chip and two putts, leaving Walter as the new Open champion.

Bernard Darwin, writing in *The Times*, predicted American golfers would dominate the Open for years to come "unless our young professionals do some hard thinking". He was right. When Xander Schauffele won the Open in 2024, he was the 46th American to take the Claret Jug across the Atlantic since Walter had started the trend 102 years earlier.

Roberto De Vicenzo

1923–2017

"What a stupid I am"

Errors committed on the golf course have cost many players victories in major championships. But Roberto De Vicenzo lost the 1968 Masters due to an error he made at the scorer's table.

Roberto, who had won the Open the previous year, bogeyed his 72nd hole and believed he had lost the tournament, unaware that Bob Goalby was three-putting for a bogey at the 17th, which put the two of them in a tie for the lead. Roberto was then called away for an interview, and without checking his card, signed it. Later, his playing partner Tommy Aaron realized he had put the Argentine down for a four at the 17th, when in fact he had made a birdie three. The rule stated that "a score higher than actually played must stand as returned". Roberto had actually shot 65 and not the 66 that he signed for. When Goalby made par at the last, Roberto's error had denied him a place in a playoff.

Later, Roberto, in a demonstration of great sportsmanship, apologized to Ike Grainger, the chairman of the rules committee, for causing him so much trouble. He went on to congratulate Goalby. "He plays so good," Roberto said, "maybe he gave me so much pressure that I lose my brain. This is my fault – nobody else's. What a stupid I am to be wrong in this wonderful tournament."

Raymond Floyd

Ray vs Lee

Raymond Floyd loved playing golf for money and in 1965, fresh off a tour win at the St Paul Open in Minnesota, he was asked by a professional gambler called Titanic Thompson if he wanted to take on a young golfer called Lee Trevino in a money match. Ray hadn't heard of Trevino but said he'd play anybody he'd never heard of for money, anywhere.

They played at Horizon Golf Club, in El Paso, a course Ray had never played. He put up $1,000 of his own money while Thompson and his driver put up another $2,000. Trevino didn't put up anything but had his own backers. Ray shot 65 and Trevino 63. Ray insisted they went again the next day and this time he shot 64, only to be beaten by another 63 from Trevino. Ray was down $2,000 and begged for one more try. Despite the person who had driven him there insisting they moved to a new course, Ray said he had become accustomed to Horizon now and so they played the third match there.

It came down to the last green. Trevino's 20-foot putt, which would have won him the money, horseshoed out and remained on the lip. Ray was sure it was going to drop, but it refused to. Ray then knocked his 18-foot putt into the heart of the hole. After three days, the pair were even and no money exchanged hands.

Bob Charles

Born 1936

Better stamina and a smaller ball

Bob Charles' victory at Royal Lytham in the 1963 Open may have been the greatest display of putting in the history of the championship. After 72 holes he was tied with Phil Rodgers at three under. The next day, Saturday, the pair played a 36-hole playoff, and in the morning round Bob needed just 11 putts in building a three-shot lead. He got up and down seven times from greenside rough or bunkers. He went on to one-putt 12 of the first 20 greens.

Bob's reasoning for his great putting display was simple. In Britain, they played the small ball back then, and he said, "It's easier to hit a small ball into a big hole than it is to hit a big ball into a small hole. It relieves a lot of the strain." He ended up winning the playoff by eight shots and in so doing became the first New Zealander to win the Open, and the first left-hander.

It was the last time Open playoffs were contested over 36 holes. With the last two rounds of the championship played on the Friday, followed by two playoff rounds on Saturday, at the trophy presentation Bob alluded to how physically exhausting the last two days had been. He later acknowledged that being fitter and leaner than Rodgers gave him an advantage in what became an endurance contest. The R&A changed the playoff format to 18 holes the following year.

Amy Alcott

Born 1956

Celebratory swim

On the whole, golfers want to avoid the water. With one exception.

In April 1988, Amy Alcott hadn't won on tour for 19 months when she played the year's first major, the Nabisco Dinah Shore, at Mission Hills, California. But come the end of the week, she broke that drought by winning the tournament, and to celebrate she and her caddie Bill Kurre jumped into what's known as Poppie's Pond at the front of the 18th green. "It was just a moment of pure excitement," Amy said later. "That's part of my personality. I said, 'What the hell.'"

Three years later she won the event for a third time, and took the tournament host, Dinah Shore, into the lake with her. Although it was another five years before another winner, Donna Andrews, repeated the act, it has now become a post-tournament ritual, as much a part of golfing tradition as the fitting of a green jacket.

"Little did I know it would become a tradition that has followed forever and ever," Amy said. Winners choose their own way of getting wet. In 1996, Patty Sheehan cartwheeled her way in, and two years later Patty Hurst cautiously waded in because she couldn't swim.

When the tournament moved in 2023, the LPGA sensibly chose a course – Carlton Woods, near Houston – that has a pond by the 18th green so the tradition can continue uninterrupted.

Tom Weiskopf

1942–2022

Don't shoot!

During the 1970s, some tour players became the subject of death threats, and around that time, Jack Nicklaus received a death threat during the Masters. He was paired in the last round with Tom Weiskopf, both of them several shots off the lead.

Tom saw Jack coming off the practice ground before their starting time dressed in identical clothes as him. Not wanting to look the same as Jack, Tom sent his wife Jeanne to the pro shop to buy a different coloured shirt.

It was then that someone approached Tom and told him that Jack had received a death threat and as a precaution some FBI agents and members of Augusta National's security team would be walking with them, just outside the ropes.

Jeanne handed Tom his new shirt on the first tee, and he changed it there and then. He had a very hairy chest and some members of the gallery whistled at the sight of it. Jack came over to Tom and said, "What in the hell are you doing?" to which Tom replied, "I just want to make sure they don't shoot the wrong guy."

"Of all the hazards,
fear is the worst."

Sam Snead

Sam Snead

Age is just a number

Sam Snead loved the Greater Greensboro Open. He won it eight times in his career, the first time at the inaugural event in 1938 when he was 25. His last victory came 27 years later when he was 52 years, 10 months and 8 days old, establishing him as the oldest winner of a PGA Tour event, a record he holds today.

There was a stellar field that week in 1965 at Sedgefield Country Club – Gary Player, Arnold Palmer, Billy Casper, Raymond Floyd and Julius Boros were all there. Many locals assumed Sam had only been invited in recognition of his seven wins at the event, and one club member was even heard to ask, "What's that old man doing here?"

On the eve of the tournament there was a banquet in Snead's honour. TV host Ed Sullivan had come down from New York to play the role of toastmaster, and at the end of the dinner he said, jokingly, "Wouldn't it be nice if old Sam could go out there and win again."

Sam interrupted the peals of laughter. "You young fellas better watch out," he said. "I might just do it."

It transpired he crushed the field by five shots, with four rounds in the 60s, and in so doing became the first man to win the same event a quarter of a century apart. It was his 82nd and final tour win.

Tom Watson

Down a Cink hole

By his own admission, Stewart Cink was the most unpopular man in golf in 2009 when he beat a 59-year-old Tom Watson in a playoff for the Open title at Turnberry.

Tom held a one-shot lead on the last hole on Sunday and hit an approach into the green that he said "was coming right down the stack". It took him back 32 years to this same hole when his 7-iron to two feet allowed him to prevail over Jack Nicklaus. In the air, he thought this shot was as good. But the ball hit a downslope at the front of the green and finished in the rough over the back.

He putted eight feet past the hole and then hit a stinker of a putt. His bogey took him into a playoff with Cink, who went on to win the Claret Jug.

That night, Tom was having dinner with his wife Hilary when Nicklaus called and commiserated with him over the unlucky bounce on the 18th green. Then he added, "But that putt, you hit it like the rest of us would have hit it, you dog."

Tom said later, "I had the greatest player in the world ringing me to console me, because he knew how I was feeling. Probably just as he felt when I chipped in to beat him to the US Open at Pebble Beach in 1982."

Phil Mickelson

Phil's take-down

In November 2018, Phil Mickelson and Tiger Woods went head-to-head in what was dubbed The Match at Shadow Creek, Las Vegas, for a winner-takes-all purse of $9 million. Phil won at the fourth extra hole but it's fair to say neither player was at their best.

Shortly after the encounter, Phil was a guest at Jordan Spieth's wedding when he was taken to task by country singer and huge golf fan Jake Owen on the quality of the entertainment served up by the two greatest players in the world at the time. "Hey Phil," said Owen, who admitted to having had a few cocktails. "You owe me $29.99 [the cost of the pay-per-view event on American television]. For wasting four hours of my life with the shittiest golf I've ever seen. You guys hype this whole thing up about the big match? You guys couldn't even make three birdies between the two of you?"

Quick as a flash, Phil reached into his back pocket and took out a wad of 100-dollar bills. "Yeah, I won 90,000 of these. Take a $100 and go f**k yourself."

When asked about the event afterwards, Phil said, "He was showing off, and I took him down."

Bobby Locke

1917–1987

Bobby beats them all

After winning the Open Championship at St Andrews in 1946, Sam Snead was invited to South Africa to play a series of exhibition matches against local hero Bobby Locke, who had tied for second in that championship. Of the 16 matches they played Bobby won 12 of them, and Snead just two. Snead was so impressed with Bobby that he suggested he play on the PGA Tour.

The American pros did not like Bobby. Jimmy Demaret called him "Muffin Face" and when he saw his hooky little swing on the practice range said, "Hey Sam, you let that swing beat you 12 times?" But it was Bobby's putting that set him apart. He won six times on the tour in 1947, one more than Ben Hogan, and by the end of the 1948 season had won 11 titles in 59 starts, including the Chicago Victory National Open by 16 shots.

In July 1949 at Royal St George's, he won the first of his four Open Championships, but a few weeks later he was banned from the PGA Tour, allegedly for reneging on playing commitments. Claude Harmon, winner of the Masters in 1948, said, "Locke was simply too good. They had to ban him." The ban was lifted in 1951, but Bobby made only a handful more appearances in America after that, devoting his time to events in Europe and South Africa.

Ben Hogan

A gripping story

Ben Hogan was considered one of the sweetest ball strikers in the game of golf, but he often suffered on the greens, particularly towards the end of his career when damage to his left eye sustained in the car accident in 1949 became more problematic.

Ben had always used the conventional reverse-overlap putting grip, but in 1957 he experimented with a new grip. In preparation for the Masters that year, Ben played a series of practice rounds with his friend Cary Middlecoff and used the ten-fingered baseball grip on the greens. After shooting two rounds in the low to mid-60s he told Middlecoff he was going to use it at Augusta.

But during another practice round on the eve of the tournament, Ben reverted to the reverse-overlap. "What the hell are you doing?" Middlecoff enquired, to which Ben replied, "I can't putt that way in front of all these people."

He was simply too embarrassed to use the new grip and ended up missing his one and only cut at Augusta in 25 starts.

He used the baseball grip again at an event in Palm Beach the following month and led after two rounds. He told *The New York Times*, "I'm satisfied with my new grip. I usually three-putt, but I didn't out there. I had eight one-putt greens."

He eventually finished third in the tournament. It's not known how long he persevered with the new grip – if at all.

Greg Norman

Unplayable

At his best, Greg Norman was pretty unstoppable, and
that was certainly the case at the Players Championship
at Sawgrass, Florida, in 1994. He opened up with a joint
course record of 63, and then shot three successive 67s
for a 72-hole total of 24 under par.

Handing over the trophy, the outgoing PGA Tour
commissioner Deane Beman, whose brainchild the
Players Championship had been, said, "There are some
records that will never be beaten. I think this is one
of them."

Greg played the first 66 holes of the tournament
without a bogey. His streak ended on the 13th hole on
Sunday when a leaf blew across his line and he missed a
nine-foot par putt. It turned out to be the only blemish
on his scorecard.

He concluded the tournament with a 9-iron to two feet
at the island green 17th, followed by another birdie at the
18th. Fuzzy Zoeller finished second, four behind. He said
afterwards, "In my 20 years out here, I don't think I've
seen a player play as well for 72 holes."

Severiano Ballesteros

Piece of cake

Billy Foster caddied for Seve Ballesteros for five years, a stint that included the final of the 1991 World Matchplay Championship at Wentworth against Nick Price. In the 13th fairway during the morning round, Seve asked Foster for a banana, but rejected it because it was yellow and he liked them black. "You cannot do a job," Seve said, angrily. "I'm a caddie, not a greengrocer," Foster replied, and threw the banana into the trees. He also had some fruit cake in the bag and offered that to Seve. Just as Price was hitting his second shot, a piece of cake went down the wrong way and Seve started coughing. Price, clearly distracted, yanked his shot into a greenside bunker.

Seve apologized and in vain asked the referee if Price could have the shot again. Up on the green, Seve made his par four, and when Price chipped out of the bunker to ten feet, Foster told Seve that he should concede his opponent's putt. "You know it makes sense," he said. "You put him off. You've got your four." But Seve refused. "No, no, no," he said. "In the fairway, I offered him a half and he refused. He must finish the hole."

Price holed his putt for a half, but the incident left Foster thinking, "You stubborn son-of-a-bitch." Seve ended up winning the match 3&2, his fifth and final victory in the event.

Billy Casper

1931–2015

Making amends

Billy Casper went into the last round of the 1966 US Open at the Olympic Club, San Francisco, three shots behind Arnold Palmer, a deficit that lengthened to seven at the turn. Billy then birdied the 12th, 15th and 16th, while Palmer made three successive bogeys from the 15th. Playing the last, they were level.

On the green, Palmer left a birdie putt four feet short, and asked Billy what he wanted him to do. "Go ahead," Billy said, intimating that he should putt out. "While you're hot." Palmer sank the putt and then the next day lost an 18-hole playoff to Billy by four shots.

For years, his sarcastic remark haunted Billy. Forty-seven years later, aged 82, he discovered he had an incurable condition called amyloidosis, and said the one thing he must do before he died was apologize to Palmer, who many claim was never the same after that US Open defeat.

At the Champions Dinner at Augusta in 2014, Billy asked Palmer if he could have a word, and they snuck off to the Champions locker room. "I'm sorry Arnie," Billy said. "I'm sorry for what I said." Palmer told him not to worry about it. He admitted losing the Open hurt, as did Billy's words. Then he said, "Who am I to judge? You've brought more joy into this old world than anyone I've ever met." Then they hugged and tears ran down Billy's face.

He died the following year of a heart attack.

"My parents were strict and taught me the proper fundamentals that I would use in my life. They taught me commitment to work hard."

Billy Casper

Pádraig Harrington

Giving it away

In 1996, having won his European Tour card a few months earlier, Pádraig Harrington was in Nairobi preparing for the Kenya Open, a Challenge Tour event, when he learned that a spot had opened up at the South African PGA Championship, a full European Tour event. Four others in the field were offered it first but they declined, so Pádraig flew to Durban. As soon as he arrived at the course he practised for 14 hours in 40-degree heat.

That night he was very sick. He was extremely dehydrated and says he should have been on a drip but with a late tee time he played the next day. He was assigned a local caddie that wouldn't talk to Pádraig if he made a bogey. He had just signed a contract with Maxfli and was playing with a new set of their irons that were four degrees too upright, meaning he had to grip them on the steel. He played terribly, but such was the brilliance of Pádraig's short game – something that stayed with him throughout his career – he got up and down at practically every hole. He made the cut, finished 48th, and won £1,460.

On the Sunday night, he called home. "Mum, you will not believe it," he said. "I played terrible. Everything went wrong this week. I finished 48th. I won £1,460. They are just giving it away."

Arnold Palmer

Over and out

Lee Trevino was interviewed back in 2017, a few months after Arnold Palmer's death, on the eve of a Champions Tour event in Missouri. He was sitting with Jack Nicklaus and Gary Player, reminiscing about the King.

About a decade earlier, Trevino said he was paired with Arnie in a Champions Tour event, the Administaff Small Business Classic, in Houston, and Arnie hit a shot that turned out to be the last competitive shot he played.

They were at the par-3 4th hole and after Arnie had hit his tee shot, he turned to Trevino and said, "How close is that?"

Trevino replied, "How close is what? The ball hit up on the bank and rolled back down into the water."

Arnie said, "What?"

"It rolled back in the water," Trevino repeated. "Arnie, the pin is on the right side. That's a tree you were shooting at over there."

Trevino said Arnie quit there and then. "That's it," Arnie said. "That's the last competitive shot I'll ever hit."

He continued playing, because Arnie said he had never walked in from a round of golf in his life, and he wasn't going to start now. But for the remainder of the round, he didn't count his strokes.

Justin Thomas

Born 1993

JT's slam dunk

When the two-times USPGA champion Justin Thomas was 15 he played a few holes of golf with one of sport's biggest stars – and took home a few thousand dollars.

Justin grew up in Louisville, Kentucky, and every year NBA giant Michael Jordan would come into town for the Kentucky Derby. Before hitting Churchill Downs, Jordan liked to play golf with NBA buddy Junior Bridgeman at Harmony Landings, the club where Justin's dad Mike was head pro.

One year, Justin was out caddying for his father when Jordan said, "Little man, go get your clubs, you're playing the last seven holes with us." Jordan and Bridgeman knew Justin was a keen golfer, but they had no idea how good he was.

Jordan and Bridgeman liked to gamble big on their matches and they put money down on this one, too. Despite feeling the pressure of playing alongside Jordan, Justin proceeded to make four birdies in the seven holes and ended up winning the money match. "I didn't know the amount [we were playing for]," Justin told Stephen Colbert on *The Late Show*. "[Jordan] told everybody not to tell me how much because [I would freak out]. But I won probably three or four grand. It helped pay for my first car."

Annika Sörenstam

A win for the kids

Annika Sörenstam had been retired for 13 years when she made a sensational return to the LPGA Tour at the Gainbridge Championship at Lake Nona, Florida, in February 2021. She was keen to play it down, saying it was "an appearance" and "not a comeback", and wouldn't have played if it hadn't been held at her home course. The following week she said she was going to go back to being a wife and a mother. But her rivals were excited at the prospect of having her in the field. Patty Tavatanakit said it gave her a "Tiger feeling" and Gaby López described it as "a dream come true", remembering the time as a young girl she had followed Annika down a fairway to get her autograph. Annika made the cut but finished last in the field at 13 over.

Six months later Annika had a wire-to-wire victory in her first appearance in the US Senior Women's Open at Brooklawn, Connecticut, winning by four shots. She said when she turned 50, she asked her children, Ava and Will, "Do you want to see Mama play?" and they said, "Yes, we want to see Mama play." They chose a good week.

Laura Davies, who finished third that week, said afterwards, "I thought she would win. She looked like the Annika of old, and she's proven it. After Day 1, I knew we were all in trouble."

Johnny Miller

Mystic Miller

In 1981, Johnny Miller was in a playoff for the Million Dollar Challenge in South Africa against Severiano Ballesteros, who was at the peak of his powers at the time. Earlier in the week, Johnny said he had had an encounter with a mystic, Rene Kurinsky, who told him he would win the tournament on one condition: that he didn't at any point wish badly for his opponent. Willing someone to miss a putt, for instance, would only send positive vibes to the other person, empowering them.

Johnny said that on about five holes of the playoff, Seve had short, very makeable putts to win the tournament, and every time, Johnny kept his mind blank, refusing to do what most people in that position would do – namely, pray that Seve would miss. And every time, Seve *did* miss.

Eventually, at the ninth extra hole, Johnny won the tournament by making a putt of his own.

Lee Trevino

Chips with everything

When Lee Trevino won the Open at Muirfield in 1972, he holed four chip shots from off the green during the week. It began on the Friday, with a chip-in from off the 2nd green. On the Saturday, Lee shot 30 on the back nine, including five successive birdies from the 14th. At the 16th, he was on a downslope in a bunker to the right of the green. His intention was to fly it 30 feet past the hole and hope the contours of the green would take it back towards the pin. Instead, he hit it on the second bounce straight into the hole. Then at the 18th, from the rough at the back edge of the green, he rolled in another chip.

The next day, on the tee at the par-5 17th, Lee was tied at six under with Tony Jacklin, with Jack Nicklaus in the clubhouse one shot behind. Lee's drive found a bunker, and three shots later he was over the back of the green. With Jacklin in the throat of the green in two, walking up the fairway, Lee said to his British rival, "It's your Open, Tony."

Only, fate had other ideas. Jacklin chipped to 15 feet, and then amazingly, Lee holed his chip and run from the back edge for a par. When Jacklin three-putted, Lee went to the final hole with a one-shot lead that he would not relinquish.

Ian Baker-Finch

Born 1960

From triumph to disaster

It's considered one of the saddest stories in golf: the rise and very sharp fall of Ian Baker-Finch. In 1991, he conquered the world, shooting 64-66 on the weekend to win the Open at Royal Birkdale. Six years later he quit the game for good.

At the Open at St Andrews in 1995, he pulled his opening drive so far left it ran across the vast expanse of fairway that comprises both the 1st and 18th holes and under the out of bounds fence. Caddies said they had never seen anyone hit it there, not even club golfers.

Ian's game reached its nadir in the 1997 Open at Royal Troon. He had missed every cut so far that season and considered pulling out, until his compatriot Peter Senior persuaded him not to. He had already let his regular caddie go, so he had tennis champion Todd Woodbridge on his bag.

He started with a par, but then things fell apart. He doubled three holes on the way out, had two more as well as a triple coming home, and signed for a 92, 21 over par. Afterwards, he and his wife Jennie retreated to the Champions Room, reserved for past winners of the Claret Jug. Together, they curled up on the floor and wept.

When he met the world's press he said, "I can't get any lower than this." The next day, he withdrew and never played in another Open.

Fred Couples

Art attack

Fred Couples is a passionate collector of art. He said as a kid he collected baseball cards and it gravitated from there. Today, his house is like an art gallery. A few years ago, he bought a Picasso, but that's not necessarily his favourite piece. A lot of the works he owns are by American artists. One of his most treasured pieces, which hangs in one of Freddie's bedrooms, is a 1962 work by Roland Peterson, the San Francisco-based painter and printmaker. He acquired it from a collector who had bought it direct from the artist in the 1960s for just $600.

He bought the last two paintings ever created by Davyd Whaley, an abstract artist from Tennessee who died in 2014. The very first painting Freddie bought, by America Martin, hangs in his hallway next to another painting by Roger Kuntz, a Southern Californian landscape artist. He owns several works by Kuntz, some from the Freeway series, a geometric series of paintings created between 1959 and 1962, and one from the Blimp series which Freddie hangs in his office. He says he buys one or two pieces a year, but never for investment. He is guided purely by what he likes. "I'm an art freak," he says.

"If you can't laugh at yourself, then how can you laugh at anybody else? I think people see the human side of you when you do that."

Payne Stewart

Bobby Jones

Master blaster

It was Bobby Jones' dream after retirement to build his own golf club and host an annual tournament for his golfing buddies. In 1931, he and Wall Street financier Clifford Roberts bought a 365-acre nursery in Augusta, Georgia, for $70,000, and hired Scottish designer Alister MacKenzie to lay out the course. Bobby hosted a tournament for club members in 1933, and then the following year expanded it, giving it the official title of the Augusta National Invitation Tournament. Unofficially, though, it was the Masters.

America was still in the grips of the Great Depression and to give the tournament traction, not only in the eyes of the general public but also among the press, Bobby announced he would be playing. The great sportswriter of the time, Grantland Rice, called it "The Emperor's Return to Battle," adding, "The one idea of this field is to beat Jones. Sport has never seen anything like this."

Bobby had no intention of making a comeback. He was simply trying to launch a tournament and finished six over par, ten behind wire-to-wire winner Horton Smith. His last appearance was in 1948, by which time the Masters was on its way to becoming one of the world's great golf tournaments.

Gene Sarazen

Lady caller

On the morning of the first round of the 1935 Masters, Gene Sarazen awoke early to find a mystery woman in his bedroom. The incident was written up in an article in the 7 April edition of the *Augusta Chronicle* that year, which claimed that Gene reached for the nearest thing he had to hand – his driver. Apparently, wielding the club, he chased the woman out of his room, down the corridor before she managed to escape. The reporters then asked Gene why he didn't pursue her further, and Gene allegedly told them because he realized at that point that he was not "properly attired to pursue the intruder through the hotel corridors".

In his book *And Then Tiger Told the Shark*, the author Don Wade says the visit was made by the woman at 4am and she was a hotel thief, after Gene's wallet. However, in another book *The Masters: A Hole by Hole History of America's Golf Classic*, author David Sowell says the woman had gone by accident into Gene's room while looking for someone else.

Whatever the truth, it didn't disturb Gene too much. That day he shot 68 which put him a shot off the lead. He went on to win the tournament in a 36-hole playoff over Craig Wood.

Adam Scott

Born 1980

Bag man wins the Masters

Adam Scott admits that if it hadn't have been for his
caddie Steve Williams he may not have won the Masters
in 2013. By the time he and Ángel Cabrera teed off on
the second playoff hole, the 10th, it was so dark it was
obvious this was going to be the last hole. After a perfect
drive, Williams told Adam it was a three-quarter 7-iron.
"You've got to get the ball back there," he said. Adam hit
it 25 feet right of the pin, the greatest iron shot of his life.

Adam says he doesn't have the best eyesight, especially
if it's dark, and he asked his caddie's opinion on the putt.
He had read it about a cup outside the right edge but
Williams, who had been on Tiger Woods' bag for three
of his Masters wins, said, "That's not even f***ing close.
It's two cups out with a bit of speed." In other words,
twice the borrow that Adam had seen. He wanted to
know if Williams was sure. "Have you seen this putt
before?" he asked. "Adam, it is absolutely two cups,"
Williams reiterated.

Adam hit it pretty hard. Had it missed it would have
gone about ten feet past. But the ball dropped into the
left centre of the hole. "It was an incredible read," Adam
said. "That's why you have a guy like Steve on the bag."

Walter Hagen

Million-dollar man

Walter Hagen's career was one of firsts: he was the first touring professional; the first to dress flashily; the first to have his own set of endorsed irons; and the first to make one million dollars.

He was also the first player to have an agent. Bob Harlow quit his job as a sports editor with Associated Press to manage Walter, and in July 1922, immediately after Walter had won his first Open at Royal St George's, he took his client on an 11-month exhibition tour around the USA with the Australian golfer Joe Kirkwood.

In all they played 120 matches, winning 104 of them against whoever coughed up $500 to take them on. Walter received a lot of criticism for his "great crusade", as it became known, because exhibition engagements meant he entered very few "open" events that year, even declining to defend his USPGA and Western Open titles.

During the 1920s, it's thought his annual income was between $50,000 and $75,000, and that over the course of his career he earned about $1.5 million.

Not bad for the son of a blacksmith, who grew up in a poor, working-class area of Rochester, New York.

Bill Rogers

Born 1951

Close call

One of the lesser-known winners of the Open Championship is Bill Rogers, whose triumph came at Royal St George's in 1981. He led from the second round, eventually winning by four shots from Bernhard Langer.

But it was a victory that nearly didn't happen – twice. Like many American golfers at the time, he didn't have any great desire to play the Open, and in 1980, when the championship was at Muirfield, he had to be persuaded to make the trip by Ben Crenshaw. "Ben was always encouraging us to experience links golf," Bill said. He ended up in a tie for 19th in what was his first Open, and after their final rounds, he and Tom Weiskopf went to watch Tom Watson's victory walk down the 18th. Weiskopf turned to Bill and said, "That could be you one of these days. You could win this tournament." Bill took the words to heart and promised to give the Open another try. He was no doubt glad that he did.

He returned the following year to Sandwich, and before their opening round, he and his caddie lost track of time. He was on the putting green when a British sportswriter, John Whitbread, told him he should be on the tee. He got there in the nick of time, just after his playing partners, Maurice Bembridge and Manuel Piñero, had hit their opening drives. "I mean, you talk about good fortune," Bill said.

Gary Player

Down a rabbit hole

For a man who liked to dress in black, Gary Player's victory in the 1974 Open at Royal Lytham is shaded in grey. He won the championship by four strokes, but there were ugly rumours attached to the victory, and which haven't gone away.

At the 17th hole on the final day, with a six-stroke lead, he hit his approach shot left of the green and into deep rough. Gary said he feared he wouldn't find the ball. But with only seconds remaining of the allotted time, during which Gary was looking on his hands and knees, his caddie Alfred "Rabbit" Dyer found it. There were claims that Rabbit had surreptitiously dropped a ball. Years later, Gary said, "They had the TV cameras on during the whole incident. For anybody to say that Rabbit dropped a ball is dreaming. I would put my life on the fact that he wouldn't do something like that."

Then at the 18th hole, Gary hit his approach over the green, and, as BBC commentator Henry Longhurst joked at the time, "into the ladies locker room". Actually, the ball finished up against the wall of the clubhouse. Gary had to play his third left-handed and he made his two practice strokes with his putter directly behind the ball, scraping the earth. People afterwards claimed it improved his lie.

His victory meant Gary had won the Open in three separate decades – 1959, 1968 and 1974.

"The formula for success is simple: practice and concentration, then more practice and more concentration."

Babe Didrikson Zaharias

Nancy Lopez

Born 1957

So near yet so far

Nancy Lopez won 48 times on the LPGA Tour, including three PGA championships, but the one major she really wanted, and which eluded her, was the US Women's Open. She came oh so close – four times. Her most agonizing miss was in 1997 at Pumpkin Ridge, in Portland, where, by a matter of inches, she missed crucial putts on the 71st and 72nd holes.

It was one of the great head-to-head duels in the history of the old championship. Nancy was three behind Alison Nicholas playing the 14th, where the latter's double bogey reduced the deficit to one.

There was still only a shot in it when Nancy stood over a 12-foot par putt on the 17th to tie the lead. Unbelievably, she left it about three inches short. "That was a tough one to take," she said afterwards.

She had another chance at the 18th, a 15-foot putt that would put her in a playoff, and for most of its journey to the hole it looked as though it would drop, but at the last moment it slid to the right and missed.

A tearful Nancy said afterwards, "'I thought it was my time to finally win a US Open." Later she called her father, Domingo, who said to his daughter, "Maybe you're not supposed to win the US Open," to which Nancy said, "No, Dad, I'm going to win it some day." But sadly, she never did.

Tom Kite

Gym bunny

It's often assumed that Tiger Woods sparked the fitness revolution in modern-day professional golf. But that's not necessarily true. Another player – not one you would associate with working out in a gym – had a similarly pivotal role about 30 years earlier: Tom Kite.

At the end of the 1970s, an Alabama-based company called Diversified Products (DP) fitted out a tractor trailer as a mobile gym and approached the PGA Tour with the idea of taking it from tournament to tournament. Before they would agree, the Tour wanted some tour players to be the subjects of a study in order to show the benefits of proper fitness training. But Tom was the only player that signed up.

The pictures of a topless Tom have since gone viral. Wearing his trademark glasses and covering his modesty in what can only be described as a black-and-white gingham loin cloth, he has his left ankle attached to some weights which he is lifting up and down.

The results of Tom's gym session had the desired effect. The Tour agreed to the presence of DP's mobile gym and it slowly began to appear at tour stops all over the USA.

Jim Furyk

Discount victory

In 2010, Jim Furyk won the Tour Championship and the
FedEx Cup – and with it a cheque for $11.35 million –
using a putter he bought from a golf discount store for
39 bucks.

A few weeks earlier, in the first three rounds of the
Deutsche Bank Championship, in Boston, Jim had taken
30, 31 and 28 putts with his belly putter. On the Sunday
night, he asked if there was a golf store nearby and he
was directed to Joe & Leigh's Discount Pro Golf Shop
in Easton.

There, store manager Mark Petrucci showed Jim into
a back room where hundreds of used putters were kept.
Petrucci said Jim spent about 45 minutes looking at
about two hundred of them. Eventually, he selected a
Yes! Sophia model that Petrucci said had a small nick in
it. It was on sale for $69 but Jim bought it for $39 because
"it's our policy to give all Ryder Cup players a discount",
Petrucci joked. After Jim had left, Petrucci told one of
his colleagues he thought it very unlikely Jim would
actually use it.

But Jim did use it – and ended up winning the Tour
Championship, and the biggest cheque of his golfing
career. Speaking to NBC afterwards, putting coach Brad
Faxon told the story of Jim's discount store purchase, and
when it was picked up by the local newspaper it briefly
made Joe & Leigh's the most famous store in Boston.

Fuzzy Zoeller

Hoop pain

Like many golfers, Fuzzy Zoeller suffered from terrible back problems throughout his career. For him, it started in high school. He played a lot of basketball for his school in New Albany, Indiana. He described himself as a decent guard – not much good in offence but a very effective defender. In his junior year, he was playing a rival school and he got called off the bench. In his first minute on court, he said he was driving towards the opposing team's basket with just one player to beat when he had his legs taken from under him. He did a three-quarter flip and landed on the back of his head. The incident tore the muscles in his lower back.

The doctor who treated him said he would have spine problems when he was older. For Fuzzy, it first flared up at the Memorial Tournament in 1979. He said he was taking his laundry to the dry cleaners and when he got out of his car and twisted his body in a certain way he fell to the ground in pain. He was taken to hospital and given a cortisone shot which he said only made the problem worse. "It's amazing I had the career I did after that," Fuzzy said.

Byron Nelson

Lord Byron

Byron Nelson's nickname for much of his career was Lord Byron and it was given him by a sportswriter after he won the Masters in 1937. It was the first of his five major championship successes, and in the first round Byron said he played the greatest round of his life. He hit every green in regulation, and every par-5 in two. That's 32 shots. But he said he didn't putt well, taking 34 blows with the short stick. At the time, his 66 was the best opening round by a Masters champion.

He followed it with rounds of 72 and 75 to drop him four behind Ralph Guldahl, but on the back nine on Sunday, Guldahl started dropping shots. After Byron birdied the 12th and eagled the 13th he was suddenly three shots to the good. He finished with a 70, two clear of Guldahl.

In the locker room afterwards, the great American sportswriter OB Keeler said Byron reminded him of a poem by Lord Byron about Napoleon's defeat at the Battle of Waterloo. Byron said he didn't know much about Lord Byron, except that he drank a lot and died young. But his father was named John Byron because his mother liked Lord Byron's works and his full name was John Byron Nelson Jr.

The next day, Keeler's story ran underneath a headline, "Lord Byron Wins Masters". And from then on, the name stuck.

Brooks Koepka

Born 1990

Best of enemies

Brooks Koepka vs Bryson DeChambeau: for over three years, it was one of the pettiest – and funniest – feuds in golf. It started at the Dubai Desert Classic in January 2019 when, without calling him out by name, Brooks criticized Bryson's slow play. "I just don't understand how it takes a minute and 20 seconds to hit a golf ball," he said. "It's not that hard."

They clashed again a year later after Brooks had shown off his physique in a magazine. "He didn't have any abs, I can tell you that," an unimpressed Bryson said afterwards. "I got some abs." Brooks responded by admitting he was two short of a six-pack and put up a picture of his then four major trophies.

In May that year, Brooks was being interviewed after his second round in the PGA Championship. He stopped when he heard Bryson's spikes scraping against the concrete nearby. He rolled his eyes to camera, and said, "I lost my train of thought, hearing that bullshit." The clip quickly went viral. Then, at a tournament a few months later, fans shouted "Brooksy" when Bryson hit a ball, causing Brooks to take to social media and thank the fans for showing him such support.

Sadly, for the rest of us, the hatchet was buried in 2023 when they were paired together in the third round of the PGA Championship and acted like old friends.

Tony Lema

1934–1966

Top Tip

In 1964, Arnold Palmer had to talk his friend Tony Lema into playing the Open at St Andrews. Despite winning three events in four weeks on the PGA Tour, Tony, like many Americans at the time, wasn't planning on making the trip to Scotland. Since Arnie was also giving the Open a miss that year Tony said he would only go if he could borrow Arnie's putter, a Tommy Armour model, and Arnie said, "I'll go you one better. Not only can you borrow my putter, but I'll arrange for my caddie, Tip Anderson, to caddie for you." Tip was based at the home of golf and had been on Arnie's bag when he won his Open titles in 1961 and 1962.

Tony had never been to Britain. He had never hit a shot on a links course. He only arrived 36 hours before the championship was due to start, giving him time for just nine holes of practice.

Rounds of 73, 68, 68 and 70 won him the Open by five shots. Afterwards, Tony credited Tip with 51 per cent of his victory and said he had followed his caddie's instructions on club and line to the letter. "It was amazing how often he put the right club in my hand," he said. Arnie returned to the Open in 1965 and made sure Tip Anderson was back on his bag.

"To have legends take you under and say, 'Hey, get your crap together now. We love you, we need you.' It meant a lot."

John Daly

John Daly

Born 1966

Last-minute champion

A little over 12 hours before the opening tee shot was due to be struck at the 1991 USPGA Championship at Crooked Stick, in Indianapolis, a little-known 25-year-old pro called John Daly was at home, 500 miles away, in Germantown, Tennessee. He was listed as ninth alternate and although eight players had pulled out, it seemed as though John was destined to be watching the championship on TV.

Then the phone rang. It was Nick Price, who said his wife had gone into labour, and he was pulling out. John threw his clubs into the car and drove through the night to Crooked Stick, arriving at about midnight. He hadn't even seen the course, much less played a practice round on it. But he was able to hire Price's usual caddie, Jeff "Squeaky" Medlin, for the week and he knew Crooked Stick quite well.

Listening to every word of advice from Squeaky, John opened with a 69, and then followed it with rounds of 67 and 69 to lead by three. Rather than spending a quiet Saturday night preparing for his final round, as most players would have done, John went to Hoosier Dome where he kicked a field goal in a pre-season game for the NFL team, the Indianapolis Colts.

The next day he shot 71 to win the championship in one of golf's great Cinderella stories.

Martin Kaymer

Born 1984

Throwing it away

In January 2015, the reigning US Open champion Martin Kaymer had a ten-shot lead with 13 holes to play in the last round of the Abu Dhabi Championship.

After rounds of 64, 67 and 65, he began the day with a seven-shot lead, which swelled to ten after three birdies in his first four holes. But then he made a double bogey on the 9th and followed it with a triple at the 13th. His lead had now evaporated, and Martin eventually signed for a 75, good enough only for third place. In front of him, the little-known Frenchman Gary Stal had put together the round of his life, carding a 65 for his first-ever tour win.

"I don't really know how to put it into words," Martin said afterwards. "It will take me a few days to reflect on this." He later said he was "glad" it happened, because he would learn from his mistakes and that would ultimately make him a better player. However, when asked what caused the capitulation, he said, "No one really wants to talk about their weaknesses. I would like to keep those for myself."

Later that year, Martin had a three-shot lead with nine holes to play in the Italian Open but lost in a playoff. Scar tissue can have a long-lasting effect on a golfer's form. Martin has not won another tournament since then.

Mark O'Meara

Defying the King

At the 1996 Presidents Cup in Gainesville, Virginia, US team captain Arnold Palmer told his players beforehand that he was going to be 100 per cent responsible for all the pairings. He didn't want any input from his team.

Mark O'Meara dared to challenge the King. He had played practice rounds with Tiger Woods and David Duval, who he said was just coming onto the scene, and although he hadn't won a lot at that point, Mark could see his potential.

Mark approached Arnie and said, "AP, give me this kid, David Duval. I promise we will not lose." Arnie lost his temper, and Mark decided to back off. Later, at a team meeting the evening before the first day's play, Arnie stood up and said, "I told you guys not to interfere with pairings, but O'Meara over there" – and he pointed at Mark – "he had to come over to me and tell me who he wanted to play with." And then according to Mark, he winked at him and said, "You're playing with David Duval."

Mark and Duval were fourth out on the first morning and beat Steve Elkington and Frank Nobilo 3&2, and then recorded further wins that afternoon and the following morning. The USA beat the International team 16½-15½.

Peter Thomson

1929–2018

Making a name for himself

Despite winning 98 times around the world, including five Open Championship titles between 1954 and 1965, American golf audiences knew little about Peter Thomson. Only his 1965 Open win at Royal Birkdale was achieved when the top American golfers had begun playing the championship again. And he had only one success on the PGA Tour – the Texas International Open in 1956 – because he would leave America at the end of July to go back to Australia.

But America learned a lot more about Peter in 1985. He won 11 Senior Tour titles in his career, but that year won an astonishing nine times – out of 24 events – and was a runaway leader at the top of the money list. His run began in March with a one-shot victory over Arnold Palmer and Billy Casper at the Vintage Invitational at Indian Wells.

It was redemption of sorts for Peter. Critics said his game wasn't suited to American courses because he wasn't a big driver of the ball. "Golf is like tennis. The game doesn't really start until the serve gets in," he said.

But he was highly respected by his peers. Jack Nicklaus said after he had missed the cut as a 17-year-old amateur at the US Open in 1957, he crawled on his hands and knees to the back of one tee just so he could watch Peter.

Dustin Johnson

Laid back DJ

Some people have called it the biggest choke in golf: after two brilliant shots to the par-5 18th, Dustin Johnson had a 12-foot putt for eagle to win the 2015 US Open at Chambers Bay, in Washington. Miss it, and he would be in a playoff the next day with Jordan Spieth. He hit his first four feet past and the return putt never threatened the hole. There were concerns DJ might never recover from this meltdown.

Later, DJ was driving back to his rented house with his then girlfriend Paulina, his caddie/brother Austin and agent David Winkle. Nobody said anything until DJ pulled off the road, turned to everyone and said, "Lighten up! Guys, it's just golf." It didn't leave any scar tissue. He won the US Open at Oakmont the following year.

Rory McIlroy describes DJ's attitude towards golf as, "See ball, hit ball. See putt, hole putt, go to the next." Sometimes his laid back approach beggars belief. At the 2020 Masters, walking down the final fairway with victory guaranteed, he turned to Austin and said, "How do we stand?" "What do you mean?" Austin replied. "In the tournament, how do we stand?" DJ asked. "How are we doing?" He had no idea where he was in relation to the field.

Austin told him he was five clear and had one arm in the green jacket. A 15-handicapper could win the Masters from here, Austin said.

Kathy Whitworth

1939–2022

Big head

At the end of the 1964 LPGA season, Kathy Whitworth, an eight-time winner the previous year, hadn't won an event and was beginning to get very down on herself. If she was to break her duck, she would have to win the San Antonio Civitan Open, in Texas, her last event of the season.

On the eve of the tournament, she went out to dinner with her old coach Hardy Loudermilk, who was the head pro at Oak Hills in San Antonio, and described her problems to him. "Sounds like you have the big head to me," Hardy said. His comment hit Kathy right between the eyes. The next day she played a practice round and still she couldn't control the ball as she wanted to. Once again, a bad attitude set in and it was then that Kathy said to herself, "Hardy's right." She realized she had been doing it all year and it had become a habit.

She was able to make a mental adjustment during the tournament and she ended up tying Mickey Wright, before going on to win the playoff. She said it was a big turning point for her. She won eight times the following year, and finished her career with 88 tour wins, the most by any pro golfer, man or woman, including six major championships. She was also the first woman to win over $1 million in prize money.

Dave Stockton

Born 1941

Fighting the Army

In 1970, Dave Stockton won the PGA Championships at Southern Hills, in Tulsa, after a fierce last round duel with a 40-year-old Arnold Palmer. At times it felt as if Dave was not only battling his more famous opponent, but the whole of his Army as well.

As Dave was preparing to hit a wedge shot at the 7th, a fan loyal to the King shouted, "Bury it in the sand, Davy." Another yelled, "Shank it." Dave did bury it – in the hole for an eagle two. At the long par-4 13th, Dave's second shot found water. "Yahoo, go get him now, Arnie," someone cried out. The hollering only fired Dave up. He said, "I wanted to hole my chip shot just for spite. I told myself if I did I would cram the ball down that guy's throat." Dave nearly did hole his chip. He knocked it stiff, limiting the damage to a bogey. "I knew I had it then. That was the shot," he said.

Before he holed his winning putt on the 18th, Dave saw his wife Kathy in the crowd and tears welled in his eyes. His caddie had to hand him a towel so he could wipe his face. "I felt sorry for Arnie," he said afterwards, "but only for one-millionth of a second."

Six years later, Dave won his second PGA title, but Arnie left the game without having ever won it.

Jack Nicklaus

No sweater, no sweat

"If you're going to be a player people will remember, you have to win the Open at St Andrews," said Jack Nicklaus towards the end of his career. He won two Opens at the home of golf, the first in 1970 in a playoff against the hapless Doug Sanders. Hapless, because the 46-year-old Georgia native missed a three-foot putt on the 72nd hole that would have won him the title.

The next day, in an 18-hole playoff, Nicklaus had a four-shot lead over Sanders after 13 holes, but by the time they came to the final hole he was only one shot to the good. As he approached the tee, he famously removed his yellow sweater and handed it to his caddie. He then hit a drive of about 360 yards, which went over the back of the green and into a collar of rough.

Sanders played the hole more conventionally, leaving himself a short putt for birdie. Jack's chip finished about 15 feet short, from where he slid the putt into the right edge of the hole. In celebration, he flung his putter in the air.

Jack had achieved his dream of winning the Open at St Andrews. As for Sanders, he said over time he became less haunted by his missed putt. "It doesn't hurt much anymore," he said in 2000. "These days I can go a full five minutes without thinking about it."

Tiger Woods

A friendly round of golf

A week before the Masters in 1997, Tiger Woods and his friend Mark O'Meara agreed to play two practice rounds together at Isleworth Golf Club, Florida, to get their games into shape for Augusta.

Starting at the 10th, Tiger played his first nine holes in nine under par. He ended up shooting 59, which could have been better had he not been distracted on the par-5 3rd hole, his 12th, by the space shuttle *Columbia* taking off from Cape Canaveral, causing him to make only a par.

The score was a course record and the scorecard hung in the clubhouse until 2004 when the course underwent renovation and the card got lost.

The next day the match lasted all of two holes. Again, starting on the back nine, Tiger birdied the 10th. At the 11th he made a hole-in-one before O'Meara had even got out of his cart.

They had been playing for money – $10 automatic one-downs – and O'Meara took $100 from his pocket and put it on Tiger's cart seat. "That was a nice shot," he said. "I quit."

When Tiger asked him where he was going O'Meara said, "You were 13 under yesterday. You're 16 under for the last 20 holes. I'm not playing golf with you anymore. I'll see you on the range when you're done."

"It was awesome. I hate that guy."

Eight days later Tiger won the Masters by 12 shots.

"Be decisive.
A wrong decision is
generally less disastrous
than indecision."

Bernhard Langer